THINKERS

50

Future Thinkers

D1115765

Future Thinkers

New Thinking on Leadership, Strategy, and Innovation for the Twenty-First Century

STUART CRAINER + DES DEARLOVE

New York   Chicago   San Francisco   Athens   London   Madrid
Mexico City   Milan   New Delhi   Singapore   Sydney   Toronto

1 2 3 4 5 6 7 8 9 0 DOC/DOC 1 2 0 9 8 7 6 5 4

ISBN   978-0-07-182749-2
MHID   0-07-182749-8

e-ISBN 978-0-07-182750-8
e-MHID   0-07-182750-1

Library of Congress Cataloging-in-Publication Data

Crainer, Stuart.
  Thinkers 50 : future thinkers : new thinking on leadership, strategy, and
innovation for the 21st century / Stuart Crainer and Des Dearlove. — 1 Edition.
    pages cm
  ISBN 978-0-07-182749-2 (paperback) — ISBN 0-07-182749-8
  1. Management. 2. Leadership. 3. Strategic planning. I. Dearlove, Des.
II. Title. III. Title: Thinkers fifty.
  HD31.C6867 2014
  658.4—dc23
                                                            2014010331

McGraw-Hill Education books are available at special quantity discounts
to use as premiums and sales promotions or for use in corporate training
programs. To contact a representative, please visit the Contact Us pages at
www.mhprofessional.com.

Contents

CONTENTS

Introduction

The science of business best practices never stands still. State-of-the-art management and leadership techniques are continually evolving. Think about it: the way organizations are run now is radically different from the way they were run just 10 years ago. Technology has clearly played a huge part in this, but the biggest driver of change in the way organizations are run is the ceaseless quest for improvement: to manage more efficiently and effectively to better achieve business results.

Improvements come from bright ideas. There is nothing quite as practical as a great idea. The ideas that inspire and influence business practitioners often have their origins in the ideas and work of the thinkers celebrated in the Thinkers50.

From blue ocean strategy to Michael Porter's five forces, from Vijay Govindarajan's reverse innovation to Richard D'Aveni's hypercompetition, great thinkers and their ideas directly affect the way companies are managed and the way businesspeople think about and practice business.

Ideas get you only so far. The acid test of management is getting things done, of course. A persistent criticism of business schools is that their graduates come laden with modern management theory but light on management practice. The value of management itself is even questioned by some. Does management make a difference? Is there a future in it?

Economists have tried to find out. Research by Nick Bloom at Stanford University and John Van Reenen at the London School of Economics studied the performance of more than 10,000 organizations in 20 countries. Those authors found that good management is indeed linked to better corporate performance as measured by productivity, profitability, growth, and survival.

They also concluded that some parts of the world are better at management than others are. American managers, for example, outperform their European counterparts, with management accounting for approximately a quarter of the 30 percent productivity lead that the United States has over Europe. Better management, then, is a competitive weapon in an increasingly global economy.

The technology giant Google has gone one step further, measuring the impact of its managers on the organization. In 2009, Google's statisticians embarked on a research initiative code-named Project Oxygen. They began analyzing performance reviews, feedback, and nominations for top-manager awards, correlating phrases, words, praise, and complaints. The result was a list of eight management traits that matter, including such mundane management maxims as "Have a clear vision and strategy for the team," "Help your employees with career development," and "Don't be a sissy: be productive and results-oriented."

The list goes on. However, what was most interesting was that the Google research found that the biggest influence on whether an employee left the company was whether that employee had a good or a bad manager. Managers also had a bigger impact on employees' performance and how they felt about their job than did any other factor.[1]

Management, then, does matter, and it follows that management ideas also matter. As *The Economist* noted: "Good management is more like a technology than merely an adjustment to circumstances. Certain management practices can be applied to many horses on many courses. Some of these are eternal, such as rewarding merit. Some are genuine innovations, such as the quality movement founded by W. Edwards Deming after the Second World War."[2]

If management is a technology, getting the next update early can be a competitive advantage, and where better to look for the next big idea than to the thinkers of the future? Not all will deliver on their early promise, of course, but it takes only one or two game-changing insights to put managers ahead.

Think of Peter Drucker, who topped the first Thinkers50 ranking in 2001. Drucker was writing about knowledge workers in the late 1960s. Best practices caught up with the great thinker's ideas only in the 1990s. Similarly, C. K. Prahalad's work on the bottom of the pyramid from the beginning of this century is still hugely influential. The most recent winner of the Thinkers50, Clay Christensen, is seeing his ideas about disruptive innovation used and applied by managers in their relentless quest for competitive advantage.

Therefore, although the Thinkers50 celebrates today's most important management thinkers, looking to the future is also part of our mission. We want to identify the thinkers who will shape the future world of business as surely as greats such as Drucker, Prahalad, and Christensen have done.

As you will see, it is quite a challenge.

Stuart Crainer and Des Dearlove
Thinkers50 Founders

CHAPTER 1

What the Future Looks Like

Where do the best business ideas come from? Fifty years ago executives largely didn't care. Businesses were managed and led in ways that were pretty similar to those that had been employed for many decades. Steadiness and consistency were the hallmarks of that period. If the question was pushed, executives of the 1960s might have pointed to the illustrious portals of the Harvard Business School, Stanford, and the like, and felt fairly confident that those schools had the answer. In their lecture theaters and seminar rooms best business practice was understood and future practice was likely to be shaped by their honed minds.

Things change.

Executives today are more keenly aware than ever before of the importance of the latest ideas, whether they are tools and techniques to improve staff retention or ways to improve the quality of their production processes. Ideas count, and executives know it.

This quest for new ideas is laudable. The trouble is that it is increasingly demanding. Management thinking is more global than ever before. A brilliant idea that could reshape a business is likely to be found in Szechuan, Santiago, or Saskatchewan. It is notable that the Thinkers50 ranking now features its first Chinese thinkers: Liu Chuanzhi, the chairman of Lenovo Group, started the business with a $24,000 loan from the Chinese government in 1984. Lenovo is now the second largest computer group in the world. Also making the list is Wang Shi, founder and chairman of Vanke, the world's largest residential home developer. Besides being a keen mountaineer who has climbed Mount Everest, he has been a visiting scholar at Harvard, led China's first and largest entrepreneur organization, is involved with a variety of philanthropic organizations, and is the author of the 2011 book *Ladder of the Soul.*

The message is simple: management thinking is no longer the preserve of the West. The last few rankings have seen an Asian invasion with the arrival of a generation of Indian-born thinkers, people such as Vijay Govindarajan, Pankaj Ghemawat, Nirmalya Kumar, Rajesh Chandy, and Anil K. Gupta.

No fewer than nine different nationalities were featured in the 2013 ranking, including thinkers from the United States, the Netherlands, Canada, Korea, China, the United Kingdom, India, and Cuba. One of the most notable success stories is Canada. It has two thinkers in the top 10—Roger Martin and Don

Tapscott—joined by Syd Finkelstein, who made the list for the first time in 2013.

Thus, the best ideas have to be sought out in previously unthought of places. Thankfully, business thinking is also no longer a male preserve. There is a growing group of impressive and influential female thinkers that includes INSEAD's Renée Mauborgne; Columbia's Rita McGrath; Linda Hill and Amy Edmondson of Harvard Business School; the Cuban-born Herminia Ibarra; Lynda Gratton of London Business School; Sheryl Sandberg, COO of Facebook and author of the 2013 book *Lean In: Women, Work, and the Will to Lead*; and former Oracle executive Liz Wiseman.

Widening Net

The net of ideas has widened, and so too has the lens through which business behavior is examined and understood. Researchers can now utilize technology to understand our behavior as never before. This has opened up a world of opportunities to better understand individual and organizational behavior as well as a host of other issues, including privacy.

For example, an analysis of changes in Google query volume for search terms related to finance reveals patterns that could be interpreted as early-warning signs of stock market moves. Tobias Preis of Warwick Business School, Helen Susannah Moat of University College London, and H. Eugene Stanley of Boston University analyzed changes in the frequency of 98 terms such as *revenue, unemployment, credit*, and *Nasdaq* in Google searches from 2004 to 2011.[1]

They found that using these changes in search volume as the basis of a trading strategy for investing in the Dow Jones Industrial Average Index could have led to substantial profit. Trading on the basis of the number of queries on Google using the keyword *debt* could have brought in returns of up to 326 percent.

"We are generating gigantic amounts of data through our everyday interactions with technology. This is opening up fascinating new possibilities for a new interdisciplinary computational social science," Tobias Preis told us.[2] Where big data meets organizational behavior we can expect insightful and practical dividends.

Beyond Categories

One of the striking things we found in compiling this book is how unwilling today's thinkers are to be neatly compartmentalized. Years ago when you talked to the Joe Bowtie strategy professor, that's exactly what you got: plain vanilla strategy. Now thinkers are not so easily contained within a single discipline or perspective. Their passions and insights are often impressively diverse. Consider some of those featured in the pages that follow: Dorie Clark used to be the spokeswoman for a presidential candidate and a divinity student. She now focuses on personal branding. The France-based Italian Gianpiero Petriglieri is a business school professor but was trained in psychiatry. Adam Grant is a Wharton professor and sometime magician.

Functional divides now mean very little. The thinkers of the future will be unashamedly eclectic, capable of looking through a wide variety of lenses. Also, jobs, products, and entire industries are converging as never before. This is having a knock-on effect on business thinking. The lines between strategy and innovation and between leadership and marketing are blurring.

The Import Business

Business ideas are and have always been imported from other disciplines and areas of study. Some sources have proved more fruitful. Managers have, for example, been learning from the military world for centuries, from Sun Tzu to Norman Schwarzkopf. This is still the case. One of the most in-demand strategy speakers in Europe is Stephen Bungay. He worked for the Boston Consulting Group and is the author of *The Most Dangerous Enemy: A History of the Battle of Britain* (2000) and *Alamein* (2002). He is a regular guest lecturer at the Defence Academy of the United Kingdom, and his *The Art of Action* (2010) lays out a coherent, holistic approach to management.

Elsewhere, Arnoud Franken has drawn lessons from the Royal Marines. The Royal Marines are the Royal Navy's 7,500-strong commando-trained amphibious infantry and are the core component of the United Kingdom's Rapid Reaction Force. Says Franken:

> For senior executives, one of the key lessons from the Royal Marines' approach to planning in the face of uncertainty is that it is not about gathering and crunching vast amounts of data, using advanced mathematical techniques to create an accurate model of the world that reduces the inherent uncertainty, and using that as a basis for developing strategy by the executive team. Neither is it about using traditional planning tools inherited from a bygone linear-thinking and efficiency-oriented era that assume the environment does not change, nor is it about skipping thinking because it is too difficult and just doing. Instead, it is about creating prepared minds and maintaining flexibility of mind and

attitude to achieve a commonly understood desired end state. It is the planning that matters, not the plan itself.

Further, in dynamic environments planning cannot be the preserve of the executive team as they are not able to understand, plan, lead, and manage in detail at the rate of change in the environment. Therefore, the planning process should not be exclusive but inclusive, drawing on the knowledge, insights, skills, and qualities of people at every level of the organization.

Franken doesn't stop with the military. He also draws on early anthropological studies. We particularly like his neat riffs on the importance of numbers:

Ever wondered why there are seven habits of effective people? Or why everything is presented in threes? Actually, it is not seven or three; it is five, plus or minus two. But where does five plus or minus two come from? Well, for that you have to go back about 40,000 years.

Take your family; to begin with there was you and your parents. That's you, father, mother—that's three. Maybe your family's larger, maybe you have siblings, maybe you have one or two sisters and brothers, which quickly makes five. Or it can be that it's you, your parents, and some grandparents, two grandfathers, two grandmothers, which makes seven.

Because we've grown up for hundreds of thousands of years in that social context, our brain is hardwired for the number seven; that's why we can remember seven names and why the most effective teams tend to have seven people in them. If you start to make it 10 people, the team becomes ineffective and inefficient. Maybe because you can't remember everyone's name, or maybe people feel left out. Again, because we're programmed for seven, if it becomes seven plus three—three belongs to a different team, and it doesn't work.

So if you are organizing a team or you want to communicate a message, use the rule five plus or minus two. Communicate your messages with three clear points and make sure your teams have seven people.

Golden Lessons

The world of sport is always a source of inspiration. One of the more interesting voices in this area comes from Alex Gregory, who is a three-time rowing world champion and won a gold medal in the coxless fours at the London Olympics in 2012. He argues that it is too easy to concentrate on perfecting your strengths rather than remedying your weaknesses:

> The more I have talked to people in the athletic world and beyond, I realized that concentrating on honing your strengths and not identifying or tackling your weaknesses is commonplace. This applies to the tennis player who habitually avoids using their weak backhand; the CEO who is great with numbers, but doesn't begin to understand how marketing works; the teacher who knows their subject inside-out but is not so good at classroom discipline.

The problem is it is so easy to work on what you are already good at. There is instant satisfaction and positive feedback with an often false belief that large steps have been made in the right direction. In fact the likelihood is that the rate of improvement is small and relatively insignificant. You do something well and strive every sinew to do it ever so slightly better. The belief is that accentuating your strengths, off-sets your weaknesses.

We are encouraged as parents and teachers that positive feedback is good and the right thing to do. This is great and something I completely agree with but it means that from a very early age we are all look-ing for this positive stimulus from others around us. We achieve this by doing and repeating actions we are good at, doing them well, making them better. The trouble is that this simply moves us even further away from what we really need to be doing to make signif-icant changes.[3]

However, broad ranging though the field is, any book requires a degree of order and structure. This collection of future thinkers is ordered as follows:

Chapter 2: The Reinvention of Leadership

The study of leadership has become a heavy intellectual indus-try, but the new generation of thinkers offers intriguing and fresh perspectives. Gianpiero Petriglieri and Lee Newman share theirs.

Chapter 3: Understanding Organizations

Companies used to be for life. No more. Now they appear fragile but remain intriguing. Christian Stadler makes sense of the twenty-first-century organization, and Ethan Mollick explores the world of middle managers and much more.

Chapter 4: Understanding Working Life

How do careers work? What's the best way to work your way up the organizational hierarchy? Monika Hamori is among the best thinkers in making sense of the reality of working life.

Chapter 5: Strategy Redux

Yesterday's discipline? Strategy has been neglected over recent years as thinkers have flocked to the field of innovation. Nonetheless, every organization requires a strategy. Laurence Capron offers help . . . and hope.

Chapter 6: Innovation Now

Innovation and technology are the twin intellectual peaks of our times. But who is saying something new and original about them? James Allworth and Navi Radjou are compelling voices in this area.

Chapter 7: Sustaining the Future

There is a lot of hype and hyperbole surrounding issues such as sustainability and corporate social responsibility. What does it really mean? Ioannis Ioannou's research brings academic rigor to the issues, and Ellen MacArthur offers a persuasive and ambitious view of the future shape of the world's economy.

Chapter 8: One and Only

In 1997 Tom Peters talked about the brand called you. Now personal branding is in the mainstream as millennials jockey for position in the workplace. Dorie Clark provides clarity to the subject of personal branding. It really is about you. Meanwhile, Adam Grant offers his unique magic.

Chapter 9: All Together Now

Where does the rise of social media leave us? Nilofer Merchant provides a clarion call to make sense of 24/7 digital reality.

CHAPTER 2

The Reinvention of Leadership

Few subjects have attracted as much attention over recent years as leadership. We have interviewed an explorer, a chef, a football player, a soccer coach, a pizza chef, a brain surgeon, a rugby legend, the developer of the world's fastest supercomputer, and a host of other entrepreneurs and senior executives on this subject.

Leadership, it seems, is universal. Gianfranco Zola, the former Italian international soccer player and Chelsea legend turned manager, summed it up when he told us: "No matter what you do, whether you are a footballer, a banker, a politician, or whatever, it is always the same. We are all human beings; we change the way we dress, but we are all human beings and the dynamics within a group are always the same. And if you understand the dynamics of handling a group well, then you just change the

11

clothes and the situation and you're still going to be successful. So I believe that if you can manage one group of people, you can be successful doing something else."

Zola, who during his illustrious football career played alongside the legendary Argentinian Diego Maradona and the Brazilian striker Careca, has moved into football management at West Ham and Watford. He noted about the transition from player to coach:

> If you want to do this job, you have to learn to think like a leader. As a footballer I realized that the mental side is very important, because you need to get rid of the idea that everyone thinks like you do. It's not like that. That has been a big realization for me. I think it's a common mistake that many, many people make. I still do it sometimes because it's such a difficult thing to overcome. I dedicate at least one hour a day to leadership. It's more important that you learn to handle the leadership issues than how to make a presentation or how to prepare for a game. These things are important, but the leadership part is more important.

Sean Fitzpatrick is a legend of international rugby. He was captain of the mighty New Zealand rugby team the All Blacks. He played 92 international matches for the All Blacks from 1986 to 1998, including a world record 63 consecutive test matches and 51 test matches as captain. He remains closely involved in rugby as an author, journalist, and pundit.

We asked him about being at the sharp end of leadership on a team such as the All Blacks. "It wasn't until I became the All Black captain that it really dawned on me what leadership was all about. I didn't feel comfortable captaining the All Blacks probably for the first two or three years. But the key advice I got when I first became captain was to lead by example. When I think about all the great leaders I've admired over the years and the people I've played under, the leaders I admired are the ones that actually did the job: fronted up and led by example. So that, for me, is the key. Another thing I learned early on was that you don't necessarily need to be liked, but you need to be respected. And how do you gain that respect? By leading by example. Leading by example is such a key ingredient in successful organizations."

When we asked Fitzpatrick how he dealt with people who weren't performing, he was characteristically forthright: "If people aren't doing their bit, we sit down and we analyze each other's performance. We talk a lot about our strengths and weaknesses, what we're good at, what we're not good at. What we did well. And we're very, very open to each other. And at the end of the day it's about giving that ultimate performance, and that involves telling you you're not good enough, that you need to get better, or you're not devoting your time. If rugby is not the number one thing in your life, you need to reassess where you're at. And if you're the star player in the team, we don't really care. We'd rather take a bit of pain and get rid of you and have a player that is totally dedicated to where we want to go to. So it's a hard-nosed business. And the players who are in our club, they know that, and it's a wonderful environment to work in."

As Fitzpatrick indicates, leadership is not a popularity contest. But it is essential.

Warming Up

What is striking about leaders in the sporting and corporate worlds is how much thought they give to the subject. They prepare as leaders as surely as the most diligent sports star prepares for action.

While interviewing Joe Jimenez, the CEO of Novartis, we asked how much work he had to do to acquire the knowledge and vocabulary of the pharmaceutical industry as a nonscientist.

When I became the head of the pharma division in 2007, I felt it was very important that I study not just our medicines but the diseases that our medicines are involved in, as well as the mechanism of the molecules that we have discovered and developed.

I had a lot of help in understanding the science in the early years. I had a tutor who would come in early in the morning before the workday. We would pick a particular disease, and he would explain how the disease progresses, what pathways are implicated in that disease, and how the pieces manage through that disease and where each one of our compounds fit in the overall management of the disease.

I found that with a lot of work, while sitting in meetings with our scientists, I was able to ask the right questions around what has been considered and what has not been considered.

It is very interesting that you can run a company like this without being a physician or a scientist as long as you understand something about the sciences and you make sure that we have the right people in the room when we are debating. We have an innovation management board where there are some of the most brilliant scientists in the world sitting at the table as we are debating whether we are going to proceed to phase 2 or phase 3 on a particular program, and I am in there with them. It is amazing how you can learn a new industry and learn the science even if you didn't grow up in that background.

Such diligent application and focused effort is common to the leaders with whom we have talked.

Our conclusion? Leadership is a potent and ever-changing combination of sensitivity to context and competence. Therefore, it is not surprising that some of the most interesting voices in the leadership arena bring in expertise from psychology and psychiatry.

Clinical Leadership

That was the first specialization of Gianpiero Petriglieri. An associate professor of organizational behavior at INSEAD, Petriglieri trained as a psychiatrist before becoming an award-winning teacher and researcher whose work bridges the domains of leadership, adult development, and experiential learning. He is also a frequent *Harvard Business Review* and *Wall Street Journal* blogger and a fast-speaking—and fast-thinking—interviewee.

> *What is particularly striking about your résumé is the move from psychiatry into management academia. It seems an unusual leap.*
>
> Lots of people ask me that: Why spend 10 years training, do all this work, and then change career? But personally I don't feel I have changed direction that much.

I have always had a passion for understanding and assisting the unfolding of human lives in social contexts. At the broadest level, all my work—whether it is research, writing, teaching, coaching, consulting, and in the past my practice as a psychotherapist—has gravitated around two endeavors. The first is to examine how people's history and aspirations, along with the dynamics of the groups and social systems they are in, affect the way they think, feel, and act in personal and professional roles. I am interested in how those forces, consciously and unconsciously, shape human *being* as well as human *becoming*. The second is to help people take their experience seriously without, however, taking it too literally so that they can make new meaning out of their experience and develop more options for dealing with it.

When I trained in psychiatry, I was very interested in groups. In Italy there's a long tradition of social psychiatry. It is one of the world centers for systemic family therapy, for example. I had witnessed my dad's work in a psychiatric treatment community growing up, and there was a lot of focus on the importance of communities in my own training, on how families, social groups, work groups, and organizations contribute to making individuals more or less sane, how they help us thrive or keep us struggling. That stayed with me.

Through my interest in groups I got to meet Jack Wood, a professor at IMD in Lausanne, who became a mentor, close friend, colleague, and coauthor and

introduced me to the British roots of systemic clinical work applied to management and organizations.
The United Kingdom has a long and lively tradition
of people who bridge the world of psychoanalysis and
the organizational world, both at the Tavistock Clinic
and at the Tavistock Institute.

Toward the end of my residency, I enrolled in a
two-year program at the Tavistock to study organizational consultation and also started my own personal
analysis. Both were instrumental in my transition out
of Italian psychiatry and into an uncertain and attrac-
tive future. I also became more involved in interpersonal approaches to clinical and organizational work,
such as transactional analysis and the work of the NTL
Institute in the United States.

After I finished my residency, I worked at IMD
as a coach and consultant in leadership development
programs and as a psychotherapist within the context
of their MBA program. Meanwhile, I read, studied,
wrote, trained more, and became familiar with the
promise and perils of being "in between," a state that
continues to fascinate and puzzle me to this day.

Those years were formative. I was working at
the boundary between clinical practice and leadership
development, and that made me aware of the need to
look at, write about, and practice leadership development with more depth and breadth, focusing both on
the richness of what we bring to work every day and
on the complexity of the organizations and communities in which we work.

In 2004 I was invited to design and teach the leadership course in the MBA program at Copenhagen Business School, where I began to experiment with bringing into the classroom some of those personal and systemic concerns. My course included both cases and a large experiential component, and its success was a big hint that I was becoming a management professor, if not a traditional one. INSEAD took an interest in me a couple of years later. I was delighted, and I had no idea of how much it would stretch and deepen and support my work since it became my professional home.

That was my trajectory so far. My interest in helping people be more effective and bring more of themselves into the workplace has remained constant. I may have changed context, but the things that make me curious or trouble me remain largely the same. People laugh when I make the joke that training in psychiatry is a great foundation for working in a business school, especially these days, when work is so personal and confusing. But it is only half a joke.

Think of the place of work in contemporary civilization. It's very central. Work organizations and businesses occupy a place in the popular imagination similar to what the church or the military did historically. Consider the figures people look up to and celebrate or blame. Who are they? CEOs and entrepreneurs. In many ways they have become beacons of virtue. We look up to them not just as exemplars of how to do well but also to point toward how to live a good life.

I'm interested in the way organizations and business schools in general, and whatever goes under the banner of leadership development in particular, function as what Jennifer Petriglieri and I have called "identity workspaces." We look at organizations not just in terms of what they make individuals *do* but also in terms of who they make people *become.*

This function has always been there. Once you would go and work for IBM, General Motors, or General Electric, and if you did well, that gave you a solid identity and a trajectory into the future, often stretching over your whole work life. These days, however, organizations and careers have changed profoundly, and that trajectory cannot be taken for granted.

Organizations are still important to many people; don't get me wrong. There is often a profound commitment, but there isn't necessarily an expectation of loyalty. In today's workplace two kinds of boundaries have become less clear. The first is the boundary between organizations and sectors. People move around more than they used to. The second is the boundary between what is personal and what is professional.

People don't necessarily expect or even desire to have their whole career in the same organization or even country. That makes work more precarious. At the same time, people want work to be an expression of who they are, of their true selves, whatever that means. That makes work more personal.

This decoupling of commitment and loyalty and this mixture of precariousness and personalization are phenomena that require us to rethink not just the relationship between organizations and individuals but also the meaning of work, leadership, and leadership development.

What does it take to have successful and meaningful careers in this context? What does it mean to lead? What does it take to lead well? And how do we help aspiring leaders do it? All my writing and teaching revolves around these questions.

How do you research these topics?

I'm a qualitative researcher. I talk to people, I spend time with them, and I try to make sense of their experience: how their inner world shapes and is shaped by their outer world.

For example, Jennifer, Jack, and I did a large study following a cohort going through an intense MBA program. We looked at their development not from the perspective of what kind of jobs they got or what they learned or didn't learn but with a focus on their identity—how their sense of who they were, where they came from, and what they wanted was affected by their business school experience.

One of the things we unearthed was the process these managers went through to *personalize* their learning—how they employed the MBA to bring who

they were closer to what they did. That study reso-
nated with many. It even won an award as the "most
important contribution to graduate management education" from the Academy of Management. I think
it was because more and more people hope that their
work will foster their personal development, help
them thrive and grow, not just get things done and
make a living.

Another thing we found was that managers who
no longer rely on their employing organizations to
provide them with a career trajectory for life often use
leadership development programs as a way to make
themselves more portable, to access and equip themselves for the kinds of uncertain and mobile careers
that are very fashionable these days.

This ties in with a study I am working on with
Isabelle Solal that is focused on what we call "nomadic
professionals." These are individuals whose mobility
often affords them valuable learning and opportunities to access leadership positions. Precisely because
of their flexibility and mobility, however, these professionals' history, mindset, and experiences are often
divorced from those of people who don't have the
opportunity to move around as much.

What we have now is a nomadic leadership elite.
Yes, Richard Sennett, a sociologist at the London
School of Economics, has written a lot about it. He
says, Look, it's a small minority, but it's a minority
that has profound cultural influence because they are

people who are celebrated and visible, so they have enormous access to opportunity.

I am fascinated by this shift because for millennia, nomads certainly weren't elite in any way, shape, or form. In fact people who moved around a lot were considered to be questionable, unacceptable, dangerous.

Isn't that why we have trouble trusting people who are part of this elite, because they travel constantly?

That's the paradox that I'm interested in. On one hand we keep telling people to move around and gather experiences because that's the only way you're going to get access to senior roles. But the kinds of prescriptions we're offering to become a leader are possibly putting you at risk when you are a leader. They make you qualified but not necessarily trusted to lead. That's the promise and peril of this zeitgeist.

Given that this elite is leading organizations, why should people feel loyalty to organizations?

There's data showing that the psychological contract between people and organizations has shifted dramatically from a relational one based on mutual commitment to a more transactional one based on an exchange of services for rewards. We're now past the generation that felt betrayed by that shift, and we have a generation that has adapted to it, saying, Well, if organizations are not prepared to show me any loyalty, why should I?

At a psychological level the chance to experience liberation in this very uncertain labor market is perhaps the biggest privilege you can have, as opposed to the vast majority of people who experience profound anxiety because they don't know how stable their jobs are or are likely to be.

Yes, if you consider that to be liberation.
Well, I think the people who can experience it as liberation are the fortunate ones, but they aren't the majority.

Another one of my interests has to do with our preoccupation with meaningful work. It's very hard to find meaning in the sense that people talk about it, as an almost romantic experience of fusion with your work. Many of us desire this meaningful employment, and at the same time we don't want the potential flip side, which is that you can be consumed.

In my research and my work with executives, however, I have found that the people who experience the most meaning at work are both liberated and committed. Their commitments don't tie them up but push them to be more themselves, to take more risk, to stay open. If you go back to psychology, it's a bit like love. Love doesn't always constrain you. Sometimes it brings you to be more who you are than you would be if you weren't with the person you love.

An increasing number of organizations say, join us because we'd like you to be more than you could be on your own. I'm interested in what it takes to make good on that promise. I don't believe it is just marketing. There is a real demand on the part of individuals, and it's only going to get larger as a new generation enters the workforce that has been raised with the idea of following their dreams.

Do people now have unrealistic expectations? Will they ultimately be disappointed?
Life is full of disappointments. The question is, what kind? A great quality of mental health comes from having survived disappointment with some learning but without having had your soul crushed. If we can help people engage with their ambitions and their ideals and then learn to suffer disappointment without losing hope, I think we're going to have very good leaders.

I don't think anyone can lead in an inspiring way if he or she is a realist. There has to be an element of idealism, of wishing and uncompromising hope. At the same time, what you don't want is leaders who, because of their burning ambition and idealism, can't deal with setbacks or aren't able to tolerate questioning or to question themselves. They are the most dangerous, the most fundamentalist leaders.

I do a lot of work with senior executives, and I always ask, How many of you stress because things aren't going in the direction you really wish them to go or aren't going there fast enough for you? And all of them raise their hands. Then I ask, How many of you beat yourself up for it, stand in front of the mirror and say maybe that's because I'm not as good a leader as I should be? And all raise their hands again.

We keep telling people that they can lead and be happy, but the reality of leadership is often different. Acknowledging the tension built into leadership may help get us leaders who are more able to accept limitations without losing aspiration.

Is there a crisis of leadership? There's always the slight suspicion that every generation throughout the ages has said there's a crisis of leadership.
I don't think there's any generation that hasn't thought that the way people led in the previous generation was strange and inadequate.

I use the metaphor of a bus. There's always been at some point for every generation a struggle for the steering wheel and new generations saying, Okay, now I want to drive the bus, and the way you're driving it isn't the way I think it should be driven, and where you're taking us isn't where we should be going. Today, however, what you see is lots of people questioning whether we should be on the bus, trying to get off the bus altogether, and trying to find new means of transportation, metaphorically speaking. We are not just questioning current leaders; we are questioning the ability of current institutions to produce and enable good leadership and good followership.

But we've had over 50 years of leadership development programs.
That's a great fascination of mine. Leadership development is one of very few industries that can chastise its

own product and continue producing it! I think the issue, frankly, is that leadership development has not changed as much as the world of work has.

Look at the way we have defined leadership for the last 30 years as the exercise of influence, as an activity, as something that the leader *does* to others. We haven't paid enough attention to leading as something that the leader does *on behalf of others*. We have looked much more at one side of the leadership relationship, which is from the leader to the follower, and we've neglected the other side, from the follower to the leader. Leadership development has a long history that goes back to World War II and military and homogeneous organizations. In that kind of organization, developing leaders means helping people rise up, distinguish themselves.

A lot of leadership development is still designed with this implicit goal in mind. But today, work and organizations are very different, as we were saying earlier. They aren't homogeneous. They are precarious; they are very personal. Therefore, leadership development can't be focused on rising up and distinguishing yourself. It has to be reoriented toward a different goal, that is, keeping people connected to themselves and others—the two connections we need for a shared purpose and direction to emerge.

This is why in my leadership development programs, where I apply these ideas and research, we focus not only on developing leaders—on helping executives get the perspectives, skills, and courage they need to lead—but on developing leadership communities as well, that is, groups of leaders who take joint ownership and responsibility for their organizations' results, structure, and culture.

Leadership communities, of course, are not always inside one organization. For many executives, the people they trust and rely on are actually peers in different organizations or in different sectors. What does it mean for an organization that these leaders are influenced by a community that is actually outside the organization? Usually we're very positive about this because we look at how these external ties open their minds, keep them connected, and create networks and opportunities for the company.

But there's a dark side again. These bonds make those leaders slightly questionable. If I'm a follower, I may be tempted to ask, Where do your commitments lie? Do they lie with me or do they lie with this group that seems to be very important to you? And so what happens is that by cultivating the outside connections leaders need to be effective, they also make it a little harder to gather trust. And as a leader if you don't have trust, you have nothing.

The conversation is moving toward your definition of leadership.

I do take issue with this idea of leadership as the ability to get others to do things that they wouldn't otherwise have done. That's a traditional definition. And I think we'd be a lot better off with a definition of leadership as having the courage, commitment, ability, and trust to articulate, embody, and help realize the story of possibility for a group of people at a point in time. That is closer to what leaders really do. First you need to have the courage to do something. You need commitment. You can't do it just for a day or two. You do need some skills, but you also need to be trusted. It is something that comes from within and is also grounded in some group at a certain point in time. If you want to be "a leader," you are no one's leader.

We know from history that people forgive leaders for murder but don't forgive them for inconsistency. The classic disappointment with charismatic leaders is that they articulate their vision so beautifully and embody it with such great purity that people think some profound transformation is going to happen. Then the realization inevitably meets constraints, and what happens is that people blame the leader.

Sometimes there's a thin line between what leaders promise and the promise that people see in their leaders. That's a very beautiful word in the English language that someone is *promising*, which can really mean both things, which is that they are promising something but we see promise in them.

For me, the view of leadership as a position and a possession—as a job or a set of skills—is quite dangerous because it doesn't prepare people for the complexity, for the depth, and for the reality of leadership. It reduces it to a title or a checklist. I'm not saying you don't need all of that, but there's a lot more to leadership than that.

Positively Leadership

Whereas Gianpiero Petriglieri takes psychiatry as the foundation of his worldview of leadership, Lee Newman's inspiration grounded in cognitive psychology and is the positive psychology movement. Before pursuing an academic career, Newman was a founder and senior manager in two technology-based start-ups in New York (Brainstorm Interactive and HR One) and worked as a management consultant with McKinsey & Company in Chicago.

As dean of Innovation and Behavior at IE Business School and dean of IE's School of Social and Behavioral Sciences, Newman suggests a new approach to leadership designed to achieve behavioral advantage—"an advantage achieved by building an organization of individuals and teams that think and perform better at all levels." He argues that sustainable competitive advantage is no longer attainable in the conventional sense but that it is possible to obtain behavioral advantage.

How do organizations confer behavioral advantage? By taking the latest research and thinking in behavioral economics and positive psychology and applying it to improve individual and organizational performance through something Newman calls "positive leadership."

There are three main elements to this. The first is mindware training, which helps leaders understand their thought processes and enables them to think better. The second element focuses on positive development which is about establishing the conditions under which people can perform at their best. Companies should, says Newman, be "identifying and harnessing the strengths of their people and teams and putting in place a positive environment in which people experience a great deal more positive than negative emotions in the course of a day at work. It's a win-win: better for the well-being of employees and better for the bottom line of the organization."

The third aspect of positive leadership that a leader needs to attend to involves behavior fitness. Leaders must ensure that they and their followers practice new and more productive behaviors on a daily basis.

As Newman notes, "It is positive because it is about helping professionals who are already performing well move up the curve toward extraordinary performance." Thus, positive leadership is "the new way forward to help companies achieve extraordinary sustainable results in the modern workplace."

We talked to Newman in Madrid. He started by talking about the disappearance of traditional notions of competitive advantage.

You talk about a new source of competitive advantage. Can you explain?

As I see it, the traditional types of competitive advantage are not really very sustainable anymore. A product or service advantage—say your company delivers products better than the competition—just doesn't last, and even information advantages where your company gets better information faster than the competition also don't last.

There's a kind of new source of sustainable advantage for companies, a *behavioral advantage*. The idea is that if you imagine a company where employees literally are able to outthink and outbehave their competition time and time again, that's an incredible advantage. It's hard to achieve, but it's even harder to copy. Although leadership is often treated as a lofty concept reserved for the few, in my view it really comes down to concrete behaviors that happen moment by moment. Leadership plays out "in the moment"—in the daily conversations, meetings, presentations, negotiations, interpersonal conflicts, and thinking and problem-solving sessions that we engage in every day in the workplace.

So that's the backdrop to positive leadership. Positive leadership is about how we can achieve this behavioral advantage, by improving performance in the moment.

What problem or challenge does positive leadership address?

The core problem it addresses is engagement. When you look at employee engagement numbers in global surveys, regardless of which one you look at, only a minority (typically 20 to 30 percent) of employees are fully engaged. Of course this is bad for the well-being of the employees and it's equally bad for the bottom line of companies.

If you think about disengagement, as an organizational "disease," and a core mission of any leader or manager to cure it, then in a sense, the profession of leadership and management is failing. We're failing as an institution. If doctors had a success rate of only 20 to 30 percent in curing basic ailments, we would be outraged.

I think the key question is, What can managers and leaders do to turn the situation around and achieve a behavioral advantage? The answer is positive leadership.

Define positive leadership. You've given us a great context and logic for why we need it, but what is it? Engagement and performance in the workplace is not an abstract thing. It's something that happens moment by moment. To achieve high levels of engagement, to solve this problem that I just mentioned, to help employees to think better in the moment and create the conditions in which peak performance can happen, something has to change. The idea is to bring the findings of behavioral science and research to bear on helping people perform at their best and to help managers create an environment in which they can do so.

The way I define positive leadership is to say that it enables high engagement and performance in three ways. The first core element is what I call mindware training, and the idea is literally to rethink the way we think in the workplace. Psychology and neuroscience have made great inroads in circumscribing a set of components that drive how we think, feel, and act. We can call these components "mindware," and science has shown quite clearly that there is a set of predictable defaults, biases, and cognitive limitations that can produce behaviors that are far less productive and effective than they otherwise could be. Our attention wanders, we tend to jump too quickly to conclusions about people and facts, and we take ownership of our early ideas and close ourselves to contradictory information and opinions.

If we can understand what those cognitive limitations, biases, and unproductive shortcuts are, we can address them through simple "rethinks" that allow us to improve our performance with very little extra time. That's the first element of positive leadership.

Can you give me an example of the first point?
Absolutely. One of the most pervasive and dangerous thinking biases is something that we talk about as narrow thinking and confirmation bias. Overall, this leads to incomplete thinking. What you see happen all the time is that people have an initial idea about how to approach the launch of a product or how to approach a situation in a meeting where there is a conflict, and what they tend to do is consider too few alternative courses of action and look for information that supports the idea they have in mind.

It turns out that that sends you down quite a slippery slope of thinking because it eliminates consideration of the kinds of things you might find that would actually go against what you are thinking. You also tend to act on that initial thought without carefully scanning the environment and looking at a range of other possibilities. You tend to own too quickly the first idea that seems reasonable.

Thus, as managers and leaders we tend to ask one-sided questions and tend to reason in a way that gets us what we want from the very beginning. But we're not aware that that's what we are doing.

I work with executives and our master's students to teach them how to "flip" their thinking and how to be more mindful in the moment so that they can catch themselves committing these types of errors before it is too late.

Mindware and retraining how we think is the first component of positive leadership. What's next?

The second part has to do with a positive environment. How can we build a positive environment in which people can perform at their best? Research shows very clearly that when the daily dose of positive relative to negative emotions that you experience is high, this has a profound impact on the quality of your behavior— how you think and behave . . . today. In the long term, if a person can maintain consistently high positivity ratios, it can boost important psychological resources such as resilience and even physical health. From a leadership standpoint, we can work to help employees reduce the impact of the negative emotions they experience every day or even convert them to positive emotions and also change the environment so that on the whole it creates more positive emotional moments and fewer negative emotional moments.

That's one piece of building a positive environment. Another has to do with changing the paradigm of development from being only about developing weaknesses to also being about helping people identify their strengths and use their strengths more in the workplace. When people use strengths to work on challenging tasks, it feels good—it creates positive emotions—and they become more engaged. In contrast, when people too frequently rely on weaknesses to meet workplace challenges, it drains them—it disengages them.

A third part of building a positive environment is also training managers to understand in concrete terms what exactly well-being is, how it is integrally linked to sustainable engagement and performance, and what kinds of things a manager can do to drive higher well-being in the workplace.

Creating a positive environment is the second part. What's the third?

The third and critical piece to pull it together is a concept I have developed called *behavioral fitness*. A person may want to improve performance based on some behavioral change, for example, becoming a better listener, doing less micromanaging, being more open to the ideas of colleagues, or changing the way she handles negative events. The motivation and intention to do those things is wonderful, but research shows that most of our attempts to change end in failure or with limited impact. We start but never finish. How do we increase the likelihood that we're going to be successful in any kind of behavioral change? Behavioral fitness is a solution to this problem.

The way I think about it is that you don't go to the gym for three days and come out physically fit. It's the same thing with training behaviors in the workplace. We need to shift the paradigm in terms of viewing our own professional development as an everyday process, not as an event. We need to think of the workplace in the same way we think about the gym.

A conflict-oriented meeting that you are going to run tomorrow morning, the negotiations you are going to have with the client in the afternoon—these are the exercise stations of the workplace. If all you do is sit on a bench and stare at a barbell, nothing happens. The same thing applies to the workplace: if you don't consider your meetings, conversations, and problem-solving sessions as opportunities to practice and improve your behaviors, no development happens. The idea is that you've got to practice the behaviors you want to improve. There is a rich and vast array of tools and techniques we can pull from the behavioral sciences to help us improve our odds of making behavioral changes happen in the workplace.

What would be an example of that? What sort of things can people actually do?
We can think of the current behaviors we would like to change in certain situations as habits. There's a whole science of how habits form and that was part of my doctoral work. We can bring this science to bear in simple techniques that help people improve the odds of making lasting change happen. There's a nice framework that's been put forward for thinking about habits as a kind of habit loop. For example, you want to

become a better listener (and your coworkers want this as well). Your current behavior might be to frequently think that you know what others are saying and interrupt them before they have finished expressing their thoughts. What triggers this behavior? Perhaps it's time pressure, perhaps overconfidence or ego; different things might trigger the behavior for different people. And why do you do it? There is some reward. Perhaps the behavior saves you time, or it strokes your ego, or gives you a sense of being smarter than others. As you repeat this behavior, in a short period the triggers, behavior, and rewards become an automated routine, a default pattern wired in reward systems and procedural learning parts of the brain.

Thus, for any change we want to make, we have to identify what the current behavior is and then make a plan for what we want the new behavior to be. To drive the change, we sometimes may have to create triggers for the new behavior, and also create rewards that incentivize us to do it. By using habit science, we can literally rewire behaviors. It's never easy, but with a structured process for doing it, the odds of success greatly increase.

Are you saying that understanding and even mapping our own behaviors is something many people haven't traditionally done?

Yes, that's exactly right. When you sign up for the gym, the trainer will ask you what you want to work on. Do you want to work on legs? Do you want to work on shoulders? Do you want to work on core muscle strength? You tell the trainer, and then the trainer designs a program for you. But the exercise program is just an idea. You've got to go to the gym and you've got to actually practice at the different stations and the different elements of your program; otherwise nothing happens.

What I'm proposing is basically the same thing for the workplace. If you have the intention of becoming a better listener, you need to identify the situations that happen daily at work in which you feel you are not a good listener, and you need a specific plan that you are going to put in place, so that when you find yourself in these moments, instead of the bad listening behavior emerging, the new and better form of listening comes out. Once you practice the new behavior, it eventually becomes your new habit, and you *are* a better listener. But motivation and intention to become a better listener on their own don't get you there.

In this new model that you are advocating, who plays the role of the fitness coach or the personal trainer?
There are three parties involved. First, someone has to work with individuals to help them identify what behaviors to change and then give them tools for making those changes happen. That's just the start. Then people need to practice in the workplace, and to practice there needs to be a safe and change-oriented, change-promoting environment. That's the role of managers. I think that managers play a key role here in establishing a culture in their teams or their

units, a modus operandi that "we are all changing," "we are all constantly improving."

There's the individual and manager training that has to happen, which I think can and should happen at business schools and in corporate training programs. Then there is a third role, a social element to this. If I'm in a safe environment and the people I'm working with know that I'm working on becoming a better listener, they can be active helpers in supporting the change process. Thus, socializing my change effort can provide a healthy and positive form of pressure and also supportive feedback. I have successfully applied this behavioral fitness methodology with masters students, with executives, and have co-designed with Juan Humberto an entire executive masters program around these concepts. It works. People recognize that in-the-moment behaviors matter to their success, and what they badly need is a way to fine-tune them. Behavioral fitness addresses this need.

We've talked about positive leadership in terms of these three elements. Does that capture it? Are there any more elements?
Yes, these are the core three, and there are scientific findings behind each of them and also emerging science-based training paradigms behind them.

Let's try to put this in context. There are lots of leadership theories. How does behavioral science fit into that? How does it alter the way we see the leadership landscape?

A lot of great work has been done over time in leadership. There are many people who have studied icons of great leadership, who have proposed different styles of leadership, and then you have models of leadership at different levels. You also have situational leadership, the idea being that we need to adapt our style based on the situation, and then you have authentic leadership, and on and on. There are myriad frameworks and models defining *what* leadership is or should be and in some cases *how* to do it. What's missing is what I call the "being able."

I think that existing frameworks provide useful ideas and concepts for people to keep in mind when they are thinking about the type of leader they want to be and the kinds of leadership activities that they want to carry out in the workplace. But the real challenge in my view is that leadership fundamentally happens in the moment. These are what I call the leader's moments of truth. So when you're in a meeting at nine-thirty in the morning and you're trying to persuade somebody to join your change effort, perhaps that person doesn't like you and doesn't want to join your change effort because he or she owns the process that you are trying to change. In that moment you have to try to bring to bear the leadership style or framework you've learned about. If it is situational leadership, you have to figure out what the situation is and what you are going to do in that moment as the leader. If you are developing a particular style, you have to figure out how to apply it or how to do it authentically. Your head may be filled with leadership best practices, and the combinations of what you should do and how to do it can be immense. The bullet points you read in the latest management article might be conceptually useful, but in this 9:30 a.m. moment of truth it is your in-the-moment ability to think and act that will determine whether you are successful. This is the being able.

What matters is being able to bring online the right behaviors in that moment. I think that that's the missing ingredient in the larger leadership landscape. To my mind, the leadership debate is centered on the what and the how. What should leaders do? What makes a great leader? How do you establish a strategic vision? How do you lead change in organizations? What are the steps? What is missing is the "being able" part, and that's where positive leadership, in particular the idea of behavioral fitness, comes in, because in my opinion leadership really happens moment by moment. You've got to be mindful; you have to work on fine-tuning your behaviors so that you have good behavioral leadership habits.

We can talk about what's necessary to create a strategic vision for your company, but where that vision you are trying to develop and communicate is actually going to happen is in a series of meetings, conversations and problem solving sessions that you have with various stakeholders over time. Those meetings are the moments of truth that will determine whether you can successfully establish a coherent vision and get others engaged in it.

But if you are not mindful enough to read the behaviors happening in the room and adjust your plan and thinking, and if you are not able to control your emotions and stay cool and clear minded, the big ideas—the whats and hows of leadership—won't happen.

To me, leadership really happens in these moments, and positive leadership, behavioral fitness in particular, is about how we make sure that our behaviors that come out in the moment are well tuned. To take a sporting analogy, think of the tennis player Rafa Nadal. Even when Nadal is out of position on the court, in a really difficult situation, his behaviors are so well tuned that he not only gets the ball back over the net but frequently wins the point.

This approach to leadership is really about how we can fine-tune our minds—the way we think, feel, speak, and act—so that when we are out of position, in the difficult situations that we face daily in the workplace, winning behaviors are our default in the same way that they are for Nadal on the court.

Do you mean that positive leadership is about raising our leadership game so that we can respond effectively in the moment?
Yes. That's right.

Because they have great technique across the range of shots, the great tennis players can also improvise. Is the same true of leadership? Do we need to grasp the basic repertoire?

Yes; that's where this idea of mindware training is so important. Essentially, what we are giving people is an understanding of the portfolio of components that literally are the basis of their thinking and behavior. Components like attention, which can be very narrow, and short-term memory, which is very limited and where we do all of our thinking. Our long-term memory is what I call the hard drive where our memory of what happened at that last client meeting is stored. There are a lot of limitations associated with all of these components, and these limitations can produce cognitive biases. By understanding and training these components, we become better able to perform in the moment.

Is this ability to improvise in the moment what marks out the great leaders? Do more successful leaders do this naturally?
There is always the debate about nature versus nurture, and it usually turns out to be a bit of both. But there are people whose default setting for these kinds of behaviors is very high already, and they might do some of these behaviors more naturally than others. But it's learnable. The critical thing, though, is that we all share the same mindware components, and even though some of us might have a bit higher ability in some components than others, we are all dealing with the same limitations.

Thus, if someone is slightly more attentive or mindful in his or her behaviors, it doesn't mean that that person doesn't have a lot of room for growth. By

making these things explicit, even the people who do
some of these things naturally have the opportunity to
learn that these are the strengths that they have, and to
use them more often and more creatively.

You mentioned mindfulness. Are you talking about, as
you say, attentiveness, the ability to read situations,
the ability to be in the moment and actually observe
what's going on around you?
Mindfulness is a key ingredient in positive leadership,
for each of the three elements that we talked about.
Mindfulness essentially comes out of the world of con-
templative processes, which dates back thousands of
years and was developed most often as part of religious
practices. But now there is hard scientific evidence
that mindfulness practice, in particular mindfulness
meditation, has enormous benefits: biological benefits
for the brain and associated behavioral benefits.

It's a critical ingredient in positive leadership.
The reason is that to perform well in the moment, to
perform at your peak in these moments of truth, you
have to have an awareness of what's going on and you
need to be focused and avoid distractions. But para-
doxically, it's not a laser focus, because when you have
a laser focus you miss a lot of things that are going on
because you're just too focused on one thing.

Mindfulness is a powerful practice where you
develop the type of awareness that is focused to elim-
inate a distraction, but it's also an open and nonjudg-
mental type of attention. The idea is that the mindful

manager or leader is more self-aware, is noticing what's going on in his and her mind and what's happening with his or her emotions in a given moment but also is acutely aware and mindful of what's happening in the room with other people. Being more mindful can allow us to catch biased behaviors and bad habits as they emerge (which facilitates mindware training), allow us to better manage the negatives and more often see the positives (which facilitates a positive environment), and allow us to more easily rewire habitual behaviors that we would like to change for the better (behavioral fitness).

You mentioned evidence that this is good for you biologically and in other ways too. Is there any evidence to suggest the sort of positive leadership and management you are advocating increases individual effectiveness?

Yes. For example, in terms of mindfulness right now science is at the level of looking at what are the effects on individuals. The kinds of things we are seeing are a thickening of the cortex of the brain, changes in certain types of synchrony in brainwaves that are associated with attention and awareness. Those are the physiological findings. There are many others, but we are also seeing behavioral changes. There's research that's come out showing that children as young as five years old who practice mindfulness in school are doing better on standardized tests.

Mindfulness has been shown to increase the capacity of short-term memory, which is one of the components of mindware that I call the whiteboard, and working memory is fundamental to your thinking. The higher the capacity of your short-term memory is, the better you are able to reason in the moment. When you are trying to figure out how to influence someone in that 9:30 a.m. meeting we talked about, the number of options you can think through carefully and clearly in your head is higher if you have higher short-term memory capacity.

The effects of your daily dose of positive and negative emotions have also been scientifically studied, and the findings are quite clear. When you experience high levels of positive relative to negative emotions, it enhances your mindware, literally. People in this "positive mode" in the moment are able to see more opportunities, are more creative, are better negotiators, and are more effective in working with others. Counterintuitively, they are also more realistic than people in negative mode, and this can allow them to bounce back more quickly from stress.

These are just a few things, but more and more research is emerging from positive psychology and more generally behavioral science that applies to workplace engagement and performance.

Can we measure the impact on the bottom line?
Is an organization full of mindful people, more positive people, or less behaviorally biased people going to be more profitable? We're not quite there yet, but we're talking about improving the basic capacities

to think and to control emotions and to perform in the moment. Science is showing that these methods improve performance in these moments, and all of our tasks and projects at work are just a sum total of many of these moments. Get it right in the moment and your tasks and projects stand to benefit.

I think it's fairly straightforward. We can extend that to say that if we can perform better in the moment by being more attentive and by having a better ability to think, a higher ability to control emotions, these abilities will manifest themselves positively in terms of better meetings, better brainstorming sessions, more innovation, higher creativity, and other things that we all associate with higher performance in organizations.

What you are describing is the additional capacity of the human mind. I'm not expecting you to quantify it precisely to the decimal point, but how much additional capacity do you think the human brain has if it were to be trained in this way? Are we at 30 percent efficiency? Are we at 60 percent? How much more is there to access?

That's a huge question. In science there's a big debate over whether the brain is fully utilized. I think the short answer, though it's an indirect answer, is that the limitations in some of these mindware components in human cognition are quite severe. If I ask people to try to remember in their short-term memory a sequence of 13 letters, typically people will get somewhere between 2 and 10.

Two to ten letters is not very much information. When you consider reasoning through competitive scenarios or interpersonal scenarios as we do at work, this is much more demanding on your short-term memory. Say I'm about to walk into a meeting and I try to think quickly whether I should compete with the guy I know is going to say negative things about me in front of the boss or whether I should let it go and be more collaborative. There are a lot of cases to be reasoned through very quickly. If we can increase that capacity just a bit, our ability to reason through these things will be quite a bit better.

If we take all of this that we have been talking about, what should a manager take away from this conversation?

That being technically good at what you do is of course important, but I think it's less important than most people think. Sustainable long-term success within an organization ultimately depends on the quality of one's behavior: how you think and how well you perform in these everyday moments that you face in the workplace.

The traditional view of the role of manager is one of designing efficient processes and keeping them on track for performance. People are what drive the processes. I think managers need to shift from this very engineering-oriented view of making processes efficient and assigning people to those processes to thinking of themselves as architects of behavior.

A manager's role is to set the conditions, the environment in which employees work, and managers should design those conditions and environments to optimize how their employees are able to think and behave. This is a different paradigm, and one that focuses on performance in the moment. This is positive leadership.

CHAPTER 3

Understanding Organizations

There is something deeply unfashionable about corporations. In a nimble, permissive age they are staid behemoths. Nonetheless, they are the engines of economic might and the source of employment for many millions of people. Corporations are alive and well whether we like it or not.

However, some are healthier than others. Seeking to better understand how corporations can and should operate is Christian Stadler, an associate professor in strategic management at the Warwick Business School in the United Kingdom. Stadler is an expert on long-term success. For the last decade he has devoted his energy to the investigation of long-living corporations and the way they grow, adapt, and consistently beat their competitors to achieve sustainable competitive advantage. Stadler is the author of the 2011 book *Enduring Success: What We Can Learn from the History of Outstanding Corporations.*

Let's talk about your book Enduring Success. *What was the main idea behind the book?*

The main idea is that companies can succeed in the long run if they're intelligently conservative. That means that they are not throwing out all the things they've learned throughout their long history, but it doesn't mean that they're just stubbornly sticking to old ways. It's a way to bring in new knowledge, but in a way that fits with what you have been doing in the past.

Tell us about the research you did for the book.

It was all European companies. The research started in 2003. With a group of eight people, we identified companies that were at least 100 years old and that outperformed the general stock exchange by at least a factor of 15 over a period of 50 years. We chose 50 years because data before that are impossible to get in Europe, and we decided to focus on large companies that are quoted on the stock exchange because that makes it possible to actually get comparable data. We were able to identify just nine companies that met all three criteria.

For each of these companies we found a second company that was facing very similar challenges. It was ideally a company from the same country, founded in the same period, and active in the same industries. These second-tier companies, so to speak, were still very good companies but not quite great. They still outperformed the stock exchange by a factor of 10 over these 50 years. The top companies, even though the criterion was a minimum of 15, all of them put together actually outperformed the stock market by more than a factor of 100 over that period. Then we used these two samples, comparing them and trying to figure out what sets the absolute champions apart from the second solid group of corporations.

What did you discover were the factors?
There were several things that we were quite surprised about. One thing, for example, that we were really surprised by is that innovation didn't matter quite as much as you would think by picking up any business magazine at the moment. It's not that these companies, which are great, don't innovate, but it's not something that distinguishes them from the second group, which are also good companies. What really distinguished the top performers was that they were extremely efficient in using ideas, in using new knowledge that they developed. That was something we were certainly not expecting.

What sorts of companies were among the nine excep-tional performers?
They're fairly well-known companies. For example, Shell, Siemens, HSBC, Glaxo, and Nokia are among

them; that might be a bit of a surprise because Nokia hasn't had particularly good years lately. Well, it's looking up a little more again, but it hasn't had very good press in the last five years. We also found in our sample that there were years in which the top companies were struggling, but they were good at turning around and eventually making it.

Take Shell, for example. If Shell is on your list of exceptional companies, what would be the second-tier company?
That's BP. It was fun in the sense that when we initially started in 2003, BP was doing very well and people often asked us, Well, did you make a mistake here? Shouldn't BP be the top company, not Shell? The data over the long term said no, and in the meantime BP had a few very challenging years, and most people don't ask this question anymore.

You mentioned intelligent conservatism. Can you expand on that and give us an idea of what that looks like and how we might recognize it?
Let me give an example. One company that almost made it onto the list of exceptional companies was Daimler. For the first 40 years its performance was up, it looked really great, and then the company had trouble and fell out of the ranking. How Daimler's troubles unfolded shows quite nicely what the problem is. What Daimler got in the mid-1980s was Edzard

Reuter as a new CEO, who came from outside the company and joined the board directly. Reuter came from a media company, Bertlesmann. He arrived on the first day at work in a Peugeot, which is telling if you work for Mercedes and doesn't necessarily guarantee a warm welcome.

Reuter was of the opinion that Mercedes didn't have a future by focusing on upmarket cars. It was true that there were certainly new challenges coming, and he decided that there needed to be a completely new and radical recipe for the company. He managed to convince the board that this was the right way to go. The CEO resigned, and Reuter became the new CEO and started to implement a conglomerate strategy, essentially bringing all sorts of companies together that didn't fit the company and did not sit well with the culture. For example, they brought defense contractors into the fold of Mercedes. If you previously worked for Mercedes, you were proud of your job producing one of the greatest cars in the world.

Suddenly in a country that has a very difficult history with World War II, you find you now work for an arms contractor. How much enthusiasm are you going to have working with people coming from the defense side in that company? It's going to be a bit limited. All these ideas that there would be great synergies across the companies didn't fit the culture of Mercedes. Lots of the acquisitions were also overpriced. Overall, this whole idea of transforming a company radically without considering where it came from just didn't work. It ended up with the director resigning and the company declaring the biggest loss in postwar German business history.

That's the opposite of intelligent conservatism. Is this a European phenomenon we're talking about, or do you think the same principles apply to other parts of the world?

In their book *Built to Last*, Jim Collins and Jerry Porras looked at American companies in the 1990s, and we see some overlaps with our findings, along with some differences. Partly I think the differences are because the whole setting in different countries is different. Partly it is also that in the end every idea we share with the outside world is somehow shaped by trends and ideas that are in the marketplace at that time. For example, the Collins and Porras book is very much in agreement when it comes to ideas about leadership. They found and I find that somebody who comes from inside the company, somebody who understands the business in all its detail, is in fact much better positioned than is somebody who comes from outside, who comes with radical new ideas; that's an area where we find great agreement.

There are other areas, including this innovation idea in which Collins and Porras see a much more radical vision of innovation being a good one for U.S. corporations. That might have to do with the whole institutional setting in the United States compared with Europe, the way the markets view a company's future value. Then there are topics that find a lot of attention in Collins and Porras book and turn out to be different for us.

For example, they talk a lot about the importance of having a great vision and the whole cultural setting that enables that great vision. We don't find that culture is a distinguishing factor between good and great companies. We do find, though, that the way you handle culture when introducing change makes a difference. To succeed, you need to consider the previous culture; you can't just ignore the old culture and do something entirely different.

More recently you wrote an article in MIT Sloan Management Review *called "Why Leaders Don't Need Charisma." That's linked to your other work. Can you explain?*

Go back to the director I talked about earlier: Edzard Reuter. I met him in 2001 for coffee in Berlin, and he is a charismatic leader if I ever met one. We sat together for about an hour or so talking about his time at Daimler. If I had not known that this was leading to the biggest loss in postwar German business, I would have been entirely convinced that this was the greatest strategy ever. He had this ability to draw you into an idea and convince you that it was right.

Why is that dangerous? In this case it's obvious. It can be positive if the idea turns out to be right, because charismatic leaders are able to take you to places where you're reluctant to go. The problem is that this might be the wrong direction and the usual sort of reluctance to look at other things is overcome more easily. It's a more risky situation if you have a charismatic leader and it turns out that big mistakes are a more substantial problem. That's why it's generally better—less risky—to rely on somebody who is a corporate insider, who is a real team player, who makes sure that everyone is engaged and on board rather than somebody who leads you to unknown territories.

What you're saying is that there's an extreme factor in the sense that when they're right, they're very, very right and brilliant. But of course the other side of that is that when they're wrong, they can be very, very wrong and do untold damage.

Exactly. Don Hambrick, who is doing a lot of research on top management teams, has done a study in which they looked at annual reports and the size of the CEO's picture in them. He looked at the premium the CEO is paid compared with the other board members, and he looked at how often in the statement the CEO uses at the front of the annual report a personal pronoun, in other words, "I and me" was used rather than "we and us." This was a way to distinguish those who are really focused on their own persona from those who are not so narcissistic, and Hambrick finds in statistical tests exactly the same volatility and extremes I described as charismatic leaders.

*Can you put your finger on what was charismatic
about the CEO you described earlier?*

It's extremely hard to put your finger on these sorts
of things, but it's almost like you're seeing the light
when you sit with somebody of that kind. The person
talks about things you haven't thought about or in a
certain way is able to trigger an enthusiasm for an idea
for which you usually wouldn't have enthusiasm. It's
impossible to really put your finger on whether this is
somebody who's born with that or somebody who is
growing into that.

If I look at Reuter, for example, he has an interesting background. His father was the most legendary
mayor that Berlin had after World War II, when there
was this struggle to keep Berlin out of the grip of the
Soviet Union. With his father, who lived in Turkey
for a while, so that Reuter grew up over there, he was
socialized into this whole field of politics. That made
him a special person, but what exactly it is, I'm not
sure why he is the way he is.

*We talked a little bit about the downside of charis-
matic leaders. What are the characteristics of the
intelligently conservative leader?*

First of all, these leaders are less flamboyant. We found
they were typically more down to earth. Almost all of
them were company men, that is, people who didn't
come from outside but spent their entire career within
the corporation. Most of them had a lot of focus and

a particular expertise as well. For example, somebody comes as an engineer in training, and that really does shape that person as a manager to the very end, and that sort of characteristic was shining through all of them.

Are there any dangers or downsides with this style of leadership?

What you might be afraid of is that somebody of that kind will not institute radical changes in a corporation. One of the people I interviewed twice was Cornelius Herkstroter, who was the CEO of Shell in the mid-1990s. Now, Herkstroter was somebody with a finance background, and I found him to be a relatively dry personality. But what was good about him being focused on these things, possibly not being somebody who was trying to do everything by himself, is that he understood some of the limitations that came with his job. The company at that time was in need of something, some sort of change. It had been lagging behind Exxon in terms of return on average capital employed, which is a key performance indicator in this industry, for all of the 1990s. Shell had around 7 percent. Typically, Exxon should be around 13 percent, so it was a substantial gap. The company understood that something needed to be done.

Now, Herkstroter initiated a fact-finding mission in which he started to talk to people on the board. The board members started talking to the level below and further, going down the organization to find out what was really the problem. You could say possibly you know what the problem is; this is an organization that was very decentralized, and whatever cost-cutting exercise you would try to implement never quite worked out. So that fundamental problem really was known. But nonetheles, having these conversations started to make people aware that something needed to change.

Was he able to make that change work?
Knowing Shell so well because he spent his entire career there, Herkstroter was able to engage with all these people. He also understood that massive structural change is not going to be possible in an organization like Shell. You can't just centralize everything. It's going to break the organization apart. It also takes away some of the advantages that you have, like being very close to local governments; that's important in the oil industry, as you would expect. So instead of introducing radical structural changes at the time, they set up a training program that was run by three teams in three different locations, running lots of people through them and making them aware of how to work less bureaucratically.

Now, in 1999 the oil price dropped below $10 a barrel. Herkstroter in the meantime had retired, and there was a new leader, Mark Moody-Stuart. And when the oil price dropped below $10 a barrel, which was radical at the time, the whole industry was in shock. This was the time when something more radical could be done.

Structural changes were introduced only after the organization had prepared itself for four years—and when there was an opportunity because of a crisis in the outside world to do something more radical. That's something that leaders who are intelligently conservative do much better in my view than charismatic leaders. They do what's doable, and they're not doing something that turns out to get stuck somewhere in a large organization, because people in the end can't really be forced to do something that is entirely against their will.

What should managers take away from your research and your ideas?

A big takeaway is not to try to do something completely new. Listen to where the organization comes from and work with that. Even though it's always cool to be somebody who introduces the big, new next thing, this is associated often with problems and difficulties. Being a bit more conservative in a time when everyone talks about innovation is actually a good thing and does pay off in the long run.

Kissing in Action

Organizations and corporations are broad churches. Ethan Mollick is the epitome of the modern business school professor. The word *eclectic* doesn't begin to cover his interests or his experiences. He is a professor of management at the Wharton School.

The focus of his research is on the ways in which an individual's actions can affect firms and industries. His research includes early-stage entrepreneurship and crowdfunding, the way in which communities of users come together to innovate, and the factors that drive the performance of entrepreneurial companies. "Part of why I was drawn to academia was an interest in the innovative, the historically fascinating, and the lyrical," he says. His website includes an entertaining section on ephemera, including details of the five great permanent tidal whirlpools in the world, the music of the spheres, and the most kissed girl in the world (answers available at www.startupinnovation.org).

Mollick is the author (with David Edery) of *Changing the Game: How Videogames Are Transforming the Future of Business* (2009). His conversation with us began on the phone in the elevator up to his office at Wharton.

Talk us through your career.

I did a mandatory stint in management consulting and then went and started a company with a college roommate. And then, having spent some time there, I thought, I don't know what I'm doing; I'll get an MBA and figure it out. During the course of the MBA program I realized that nobody seems to know what they're doing, so I thought I should study this. That's the journey I took.

My research is all on innovation, entrepreneurship, new technologies, and how they influence the way people work.

You take a deliberately counterintuitive view. The work you've done on the importance of middle managers is an example.

You talk to economists and sociologists and they're really interested in large-scale systems, whereas other academics focus on individual action and feeling. I'm interested in the world in between the two, the mezzo-world between macro and micro. Things become messy when you actually get to thinking about how people affect systems. That's been my interest: How do things happen when people and organizations interact?

What about your early experience with the business you started with your college roommate? What happened to that business?

He was the technical guy, I was the sales guy, and we ended up being very successful. If you used the *Financial Times*, *Wall Street Journal*, or *New York Times* in the late 1990s, the thing that was asking you for your user name and password was our software. So for a while we were the thing that powered online publishing on the Internet. The company was eventually sold off in 2006. It was a really useful and interesting learning experience, and the company did quite well for us as well.

And then you wanted to plug the gaps in your knowledge?

Yes. We started the company during the first Internet boom. I was at grad school during most of the time in the 2000s when it was all real estate, and the Internet wasn't part of it, and now it's crazy to see the start-ups happening. We went from about 1 percent of the MBA class starting companies after leaving to 7 percent last year, so it's really a booming area.

My interest was really in entrepreneurship. A lot of the advice entrepreneurs are given is written as the accumulated wisdom of managers with not a lot of data supporting it. I was really interested in going out and trying to figure out what's actually happening. Is the conventional wisdom right? That was part of the motivation to do research on middle managers, who I think don't get enough attention, and that's part of why I looked at games early on and why I've been looking at crowdfunding.

Your thesis was on innovations from the underground.
It looked at hackers and hacker groups. It meant that in the acknowledgments I had to thank people with names like Dildog and Big Boss because I didn't know what their real names were, which I think is relatively unusual.

What's the golden thread that runs through it,
do you think?
The reason I wanted to look at entrepreneurship and all these other topics is that I'm really interested in how individuals can make a difference. I'm certainly interested in the social side—How do you solve poverty? How do you make a difference to the community?—but actually in the world of organizations, in

the world of start-ups and companies, how do individuals actually make things different? We tend to view organizations as these large, grinding things, but in reality there are all kinds of interesting, innovative activities happening; people are self-organizing and solving problems. How do the tools that we have make work more interesting and give people more control over themselves and their ideas?

How do you hope that your work influences executives or small businesses?
A lot of this is about encouraging people to realize that people aren't interchangeable cogs and that understanding how they're different and how to use them can actually lead to a huge amount of success. We tend to pay attention only to people like CEOs, and all the evidence shows that CEOs don't actually make that much of a difference to a company. In contrast, middle managers get mocked. The innovation isn't seen to come from inside a company; all the evidence shows it's outside.

The conventional perspective on what a company is and who matters in it seems stuck in the mid-twentieth century. These things have changed, but we haven't really updated management to deal with all those issues.

Is there any sense that management is being updated? Many people such as Gary Hamel and others are calling for management to be overhauled as well.

I spend a lot of time in science work, and the science world is always a bit countercultural. You have companies like Zappos with very different ways of running their organization. You have experiments in radical transparency, and there's a throw-the-baby-out-with-the-bathwater approach. How do you change management? It tends to be incremental because it's very hard to change large companies.

The question is how you can cross-pollinate, and I think that the answer actually is about how we can use technology to help do that. People come together and do these extraordinary things. Let me give you a quick quiz. Can you guess what percent of VC-backed companies in the United States have female cofounders?

Fifteen?
No, 1.6 percent, a startlingly low number. Forty percent of U.S. businesses are run by female owners, and so 1.6 percent is a really small number. If you believe ideas are everywhere in organizations, if they're everywhere across countries and across socioeconomic backgrounds, we're doing a very bad job of exploiting the full set of innovation available to us.

And that applies to middle managers as well?
Middle managers are like cogs in a machine. In the process of overhauling management, people tend to not be aware that everybody is essentially valuable. How do we use them and let them achieve the best possible outcome?

*There's a great Tom Peters quote from the 1990s that
middle managers are cooked geese. Management
and middle managers especially get a very bad
press. Why is that, do you think?*

Why they're important is why they get a bad press.
Middle managers have these very unenviable positions of representing management to labor, to lower
echelons of the organization, so they have to translate
high policy that they don't have control over down to
people who have to actually enact it. And from the
senior perspective, middle managers represent the
complaints and needs of the lower tiers of the workforce and translate that upward.

For their employees who work under them middle managers never have enough resources, never have
the control that they might hope to have, and for the
senior people they're not always executing like robots,
as they want them to. The whole organizational goal
is about distributing scarce resources and scarce attention, and middle managers don't have control over
those resources and that attention, and so it's a really
tough position to be in. It's built to be hated.

*What kind of feedback do you get to your research
from middle managers, CEOs, or senior managers?*
You get nods of agreement, but there's the usual bias
that people think they are different. The funny thing is
that there's really nice research by Antoinette Schoar of
MIT and Marianne Bertrand.[1] It looks at the impact
of who your CEO is in the company, and basically

only 2 percent of company performance is determined by the CEO. But if you talk to CEOs, they're never going to believe that.

Where is your research on middle managers going next?

What I've been working on is trying to understand how individuals flow through organizations. Imagine putting trackers on the top employees coming out of Wharton, people who are essentially heading for top management roles. We've been doing some very detailed career survey work, looking at every job they have, how much they earn in each job, and how many people they manage. We're trying to get a sense of how people get promoted, how people move, and what sorts of jobs people are going through.

I'm working with my Wharton colleague Matthew Bidwell. We have a study where we look at when people move up in organizations and when they move laterally. We found that lateral moves tend to be tied to higher pay but not greater responsibility. Most of the moves up the career ladder happen inside organizations, which further emphasizes the importance of getting the timing right and making sure you're promoting people at the right pace so that they don't get frustrated and leave but also making sure that they are rewarded in the role that they have and identifying the best possible people.

I've also been doing projects on things like games, which is an area of interest of mine, trying to understand how that can be used to measure and motivate as well. It's going at it from multiple sides, and I think there's still a lot of work to be done in the area.

Stew Friedman at Wharton has written a book, Baby Bust, *which is about your research into what's happened with Wharton's alumni.*

Yes, he's done this, basically a two classes' comparison. And what we did was we asked all 36,000 alumni to tell us basically step-by-step what's happened in the space of their careers. It's all interesting stuff. A total of 25 percent of Wharton MBAs have a stint in entrepreneurship, though only a couple of percent want to do it right away. It's something that happens later in people's careers. People's careers are pretty diverse; lots of interesting stuff happens.

The role of entrepreneurship at business school has always seemed a bit strange because although 7 percent of MBA students go on to be entrepreneurs when they leave, it's still a very low number.

Maybe half our class of 360 have gone on to the entrepreneurship class. If you ask people what's the chance of them being an entrepreneur five years out, basically everyone strongly agrees he or she is going to be an entrepreneur. For a lot of people this is their goal in life, and then they start getting job offers from BlackRock or whoever else, and it begins to get very hard to become an entrepreneur, to justify that against other things.

People eventually end up there—20 to 25 percent of the class will have a stint in entrepreneurship—and if you're career switching, it might give you some confidence about what to do. I also think entrepreneurship could be taught a lot more than people think it can be, and so there's value in having it in an MBA program.

What about your work around crowdfunding?
I'm interested in how individuals matter and how you use technology and tools to make this work. Crowdfunding was a natural thing for me, and it turns out that the United States was passing laws legalizing crowdfunding for equity as opposed to crowdfunding for rewards.

I've done studies with different people on crowdfunding. I have looked at the fact that crowdfunding tends to have very little fraud. Less than 1 percent of the amount of money going into large crowdfunding projects seems to be fraudulent, which is amazing because it's entirely unregulated. There are some really interesting Internet principles at work there.

Then I've done work looking at who does crowdfunding and found that it's more democratic in a lot of ways. I've done some work looking at what happens long term in crowdfunding. I was able to show—with Venkat Kuppuswamy of UNC—that 90 percent of successful large crowdfunding projects turn into ongoing businesses.

Crowdfunding goes way back, doesn't it? The construction of the Statue of Liberty was effectively crowdfunded.

Exactly, and actually it's even earlier than that. In the 1700s all the early balloon flights were done by subscription. It's an old tradition, and it's just reached new ground here.

Why is there very little fraud in crowdfunding? Is it the sense of the Internet community and goodwill within that?

I wish! The Internet is a terrible place full of evil people! I think it's in large part due to something called Linus's law, which is named after Linus Torvalds, the inventor of Linux. Linus's law says that with enough eyes, all bugs are shallow. If enough people look at a problem, to someone it will be trivial, and the result is that this gets rid of fraud.

Let me give you an example. There was a famously fraudulent project, a start-up for Kobe beef jerky. Kobe beef is a very fancy beef from Japan. The start-up was charging something like $20 for an order of beef jerky, not so much money to spend that people would become nervous. They registered all these fake accounts and contributed to discussion pages saying how wonderful this Kobe beef jerky was. It raised a couple of hundred thousand dollars quite quickly.

And then people started coming on the site and saying, I have worked with Kobe before, and every cow has an ID number. What ID number is it you're using? And somebody else said, Hey, I make jerky, and jerky has to be made of really lean beef and Kobe beef is famous for being very fatty. How are you dealing with that? Someone else said, Hey, I just read this article that there were 2,000 pounds of Kobe beef imported in the United States last year. How are you going to have enough to fulfill all of the demands? And because of these things holes started to get poked so that eventually the project collapsed. A VC [venture capitalist] with a law firm going through due diligence would not necessarily have found these issues unless he or she talked to someone who knew Kobe beef or beef jerky.

The interesting thing is that with enough eyes on these things you actually can get the right set of people discussing it in the right way. You can trust one expert or the wisdom of many people, and all my evidence seems to show that the crowd is actually pretty good. You do better with crowdfunding if you show a plan. You do better if you have an outside endorsement. These are all things that venture capitalists look for as well.

You're involved in all these areas of research.
Yes. I'm not trying to follow the hot area. I'm drawn to areas where we don't have the data, where lots of people are saying things that may or may not be correct but sound plausible, and it's all about conventional wisdom.

Is there a master plan to your work?
I feel that as I'm talking, I'm getting more scattered, not less!

But we often talk to academics who know fundamentally that they've got a 5-year plan or a 10-year plan sometimes.
When I look at business academia and the journals, the Internet barely comes up except as a research tool. The world of work is changing rapidly because of technology, and our research lags there. In some ways I'm pursuing the ideas that we are far behind, that there are lots of things we need to know more about and give good advice about, and that that's the job of academics.

Although I'm interested in building management theory, I'm very interested in trying to understand how things are changing. How can we make life better for all the people who work, increasing productivity and performance but also the ability to make a difference to the world's environment? I'm interested in abstract theory, but I think the theory is a tool for getting better understanding.

CHAPTER 4

Understanding Working Life

How do you succeed in an organization? Years ago, in the increasingly distant corporate era, the route to success required aptitude and steady competence as well as a large supply of patience. Rising through the corporate ranks took time, an entire career. That was back when a career resembled a ladder with regular promotions forming the rungs. Those days are gone.

Exactly what has replaced the career ladder is less clear. At times modern organizational life seems to have more in common with an obstacle race. Organizational charts are increasingly unreliable indicators of what is really going on. The pursuit of the best way to organize a business has taken managers through a bewildering array of structures. New organizational forms emerge with regularity; most are impractical or ethereal.

In the beginning there was hierarchy. A Greek called Dionysius the Areopagite introduced the concept of hierarchy over 1,500 years ago. The word literally means "to rule through the sacred." Dionysius—not the mythological wine lover—said that heaven was hierarchically organized. The source of this knowledge is lost in the mists of time. He also argued that the celestial structure had exactly nine levels: God was the CEO, the archangels acted as the top-management team, and Jesus Christ was in a staff position to the right of God. According to the Areopagite, hell is also hierarchically organized with nine layers. The entire structure is turned upside down, however, with purgatory as the prime motivator to climb the ladder.

Hierarchy continues its hold on organizational life, though it is a little different these days. Jack Welch, the former CEO of GE, observed that hierarchy is an organization with "its face toward the CEO and its ass toward the customer." The view may be familiar.

Hierarchy is no longer regarded as the best way to manage, and hierarchical position is no longer enough to shield an incompetent leader. Steadiness, the ability to stick with it, is now deemed somewhat less important than it once was. Instead, working life in the twenty-first century is fraught with uncertainty and complexity in equal measure. So how do you navigate the organizational chicanes of the twenty-first century?

One of the surest guides through the modern career labyrinth is Monika Hamori. Hungarian-born with a PhD from the Wharton School, Hamori has been recognized as one of the world's leading business school professors under the age of 40. A professor at Madrid's IE Business School, Hamori focuses her research on the realities of the job market. Her *Harvard Business*

Review articles have looked at why young managers are perpetually looking for other jobs, common career fallacies, and the route to the most senior jobs. She has also looked at what she calls "the CEO experience trap."

What first interested you in the subject of career paths?
My first piece of research as a PhD student back in 2000 looked at the impact executive search firms have on career paths. At that time there was hardly any research on executive search firms. I think researchers just assumed that they didn't really matter, but this is not true, and since 2000 other researchers have looked at search firms, too.

Overall, we find that executive search firms have a very beneficial impact on executive careers when they mediate a job move. Normally they can bargain for better pay for executives, for example, especially the most prestigious executive search firms.

What did your research discover? What impact do headhunters and executive search firms have on career paths?
My research has found that executive search firms are more likely to move the executives they represent to larger companies and also to the more admired, that is, more reputable, companies. Maybe this is because they are more effective in representing the skills and abilities of those executives.

However, interestingly, I also find that you cannot use these executive search firms for all types of moves. For example, they are less likely to move top executives to very novel, very different roles. They are a lot less likely to mediate moves across different job functions or across different industries or product divisions, for instance. Thus, it's harder for an executive to move, say, from marketing to sales through an executive search firm. These moves are more commonly done inside the organization.

The original 2005 Harvard Business Review *article you wrote with Peter Cappelli based on that research was called "The New Road to the Top." What were the major findings?*

In this piece of research, Peter and I looked at the top 10 executives in Fortune 100 companies, the 100 largest companies in the United States, and compared the careers of those executives across two time points. The first time point was 1980, the year before a recession in the United States, and the second time point was 2001. We identified three major changes.

First, we found that across 1980 and 2001, there was increasing diversity in the top executive ranks. In 1980 zero percent of top executive positions were filled by women, but by 2001 this had jumped to 11 percent. However, most of the female executives still filled the so-called second-tier positions. In other words, they were a lot less likely than their male counterparts to become CEOs or even to become the chairperson of a company and more likely to be senior vice president or executive vice president.

The second trend we found was the higher educational level of the executives. Compared with 1980, executives in 2001 had more years of education and were a lot more likely to have graduate degrees. In 1980, 46 percent of these executives had graduate degrees; that jumped to 62 percent by 2001.

We also found changes in the educational institutions. Between 1980 and 2001, we saw a drop in the proportion of private, non–Ivy League universities and a corresponding jump in the proportion of public universities.

Finally, the third big trend that we saw across the two time periods was different career patterns. As could probably be expected, we saw a change in the level of attachment of these executives to their organizations. By 2001, there were fewer executives who were so-called lifers, executives who started their career at the company they were now leading. We also found that executives had shorter tenures with their current organizations. In 1980, this was about 20 years, and it dropped to 15 years, which is a considerable drop in 21 years' time.

The 2001 executive population had more diversity, more education, and less organizational loyalty than did executives in 1980. Then you revisited and updated that study in a 2014 Harvard Business Review *article written with Peter Cappelli and Rocio Bonet. What prompted you to want to do that?*
After 2001 there was a landmark event. That was the 2008 financial crisis, which was the biggest cri-

sis in the last 70 years—since the Great Depression of the 1930s—and one of the longest crises as well. We wanted to see how executive careers have changed since this crisis.

What did you find? Are the three trends continuing?
Some of these trends have definitely continued. We see even greater diversity in the top executive ranks. In 2001, we had 11 percent women, and now close to 18 percent of the top executive ranks in the largest U.S. companies are occupied by women. That's a considerable jump. Unfortunately, you still see most of the female executives in the second-tier executive positions, that is, holding executive vice president, senior vice president or chief financial officer, and chief diversity officer roles. You are less likely to see them in the tier-one positions.

What about the other significant findings from the new research?
The other one is that the diversity isn't coming only from an increase in female executives; we also see more executives who were educated outside the United States. Some 11 percent of our executives said they received their first degree from a university outside the United States. But don't expect too much national diversity among top executives because almost 80 percent of these foreigners are English speakers. In other words, they come from the United Kingdom, Canada, or Australia.

Diversity continued to increase between 2001 and 2011. At the same time, other trends that we observed between 1980 and 2001 reversed, in particular, the attachment of executives to their current corporations. Between 2001 and 2011, we found that first of all, executives took a longer time to reach their current positions, and so their time to the top increased while their promotion velocity decreased.

Second, executives have a longer tenure with their current corporations than they did in 2001. Their career path slowed down a little as a result of the crisis, and once again, we saw increasing attachment to corporations. This may sound counterintuitive, but this finding is consistent with what other research had found: in crisis times, companies are more likely to promote their own employees internally rather than going to the external labor market.

Presumably, too, people are more inclined to stay put and less inclined to jump ship in a recession.
Yes, that's also part of the story. During a crisis, executives are probably less likely to risk a career move. However, in terms of the demand side, corporations are less likely to hire from the outside. There was a survey published by CareerXroads that showed that the proportion of external hires decreased during crisis years. It decreased during the 2001–2002 crisis in the United States and again between 2008 and 2011.

What about education? What did you find there?
The trend continued. We saw higher education levels and more graduate degrees. We see the same type of

democratization of educational institutions that we observed between 1980 and 2001. There have been no major changes. The trends that started between 1980 and 2001 pretty much continued to 2011 as well.

If you had to step back and characterize the career landscape that we now see, how would you describe it compared with what you were finding in 2001?

There are two characteristics that jump to my mind. One of them is that it is increasingly uncertain. In the last 10 years or so, we've had two financial crises: the 2001 recession and the 2008 crisis. The second one shattered the labor market prospects for Generation Y employees (those born after 1980).

Research on earlier crises shows that if you start your career in a crisis year, you will have a considerable disadvantage in the labor market in terms of job opportunities but also in terms of starting pay or pay levels and will have a really hard time making up for these disadvantages.

The second characteristic is that the labor market is increasingly mediated; by mediated, I mean that we see an increasing number of labor market intermediaries. In the new career landscape, these intermediaries mediate the job matches between individuals and hiring organizations. Fifteen years ago sending your résumé and your application to a printed job ad was the most common way to apply for a job. It is really a thing of the past now.

Today people increasingly find jobs through social networks such as LinkedIn or maybe, to a lesser extent, through Facebook. Employers also use these social networks to attract and screen candidates.

How has the advent of social media had an impact on careers?

This is a very interesting new development in the career landscape because social media sites such as LinkedIn bring new biases to the way individuals are matched with hiring organizations. If you do a search on LinkedIn for the individuals who would be available for a job opening, you see that LinkedIn ranks search results. The individuals who end up at the beginning of that search results list have a lot higher visibility for employers and will get the most job opportunities. It will be interesting to see what this means for their career prospects.

This research was in the Fortune 100 companies. Can you generalize to other parts of the world?

This particular research study is confined to the United States, but in another study I did take a look at the very top jobs in Europe and the United States at the CEO level. I researched the 500 CEOs of the Financial Times Europe 500 and the Standard & Poor's 500 in the United States. Interestingly, you would think, maybe, that there are big differences in the career paths of these CEOs, but I didn't find any marked differences.

Most interestingly, I didn't find any differences in terms of job-hopping patterns. It turns out that European CEOs are even less loyal to their corporations than are U.S. CEOs. This trend is probably mostly due to the representation of Eastern European companies in the Financial Times Europe 500. Some Russian CEOs were just over 30 years old in the data set. European CEOs are somewhat more mobile than their U.S. counterparts. It's very much counter to what people expect.

Another important trend was that European executives have a lot more international experience than do their U.S. counterparts. The U.S. executives are still a lot more likely to have spent their entire career in America and are a lot less exposed to other countries than are their European counterparts.

Does your research allow you to make judgments about which companies manage careers well?
The companies that manage careers well will be the ones that offer more geographically diverse positions and can rotate individuals across job functions. Large multinational, multidivisional companies such as General Electric can provide those sorts of career development opportunities.

The second characteristic that companies that manage careers very well should provide is exposing individuals to jobs with a high degree of responsibility. About three years ago, I conducted a survey among young, highly skilled employees, and I asked them what career development opportunities they found the most important for their career. The top spot was occupied by positions that provided high-stakes jobs; these are jobs or tasks that provide a high degree of responsibility and jobs with very clear accountability.

When managers read your Harvard Business Review *articles and your forthcoming book, what lessons can they take away in terms of their own careers?*

I think there are three things that may be important for them. The first piece of advice is to invest in your own education and find the best educational institution you can. Do your best to go to the Ivy League or to other institutions of high prestige, because despite the democratization of education that I have just talked about, affiliation with reputable universities makes a difference. Our research shows that the top executives in the Fortune 100 still disproportionately come from the so-called Ivy League universities in the United States: the eight most prestigious universities. Very interestingly, that is especially true of tier-one positions. The current CEOs and chairs of the Fortune 100 companies are even more disproportionately likely to come from Ivy League institutions.

What does this mean? Interestingly, at the moment you graduate from university, your career path is partly decided for you. If you come from an Ivy League university, your chances of becoming a CEO 20 or 30 years later are much greater than they are if you come from another type of university. By the way, this is even truer for executives who don't climb the internal career ladder but are recruited for a top-tier position from the outside.

My first piece of advice would be to invest in education at a reputable institution. Second, we found that executives who embark on a narrow functional career path—as finance, legal, or human resource management experts, for example—ascend to the top executive ranks faster. However, they are unlikely to get to a tier-one position. For the tier-one positions, you need general managerial experience. Executives in a general managerial career track normally take longer to reach the top echelon, but general managerial experience is needed to ascend to a tier-one position.

The second piece of advice is to be patient and invest time in gaining general management experience.

We found that both in 2001 and in 2011 the executives at the helm of Fortune 100 companies don't have a lot of different employers; they have worked for fewer than three organizations. The third piece of advice is to have a balance between external and internal career moves. Internal career moves are just as important as external ones. Don't build your career exclusively by jumping from one employer to another.

Are you saying that the top-tier people are on a different career trajectory, a different career path, from the very beginning?

Exactly. Often people have a head start that is determined by the type of education they get. Ivy League graduates are disproportionately represented in the top tier positions of the Fortune 100 companies. Definitely, your education matters a great deal. Second, the executives who end up in tier-one positions receive their general management training early on: they are rotated across functions, product divisions, or geographies at an early career stage. They are less likely to embark on a narrow functional career path.

Do you think they self-manage that or do you think the organization has already identified them as having high potential? Are they put in a different career hopper from the start?

The organizations definitely manage that. The largest companies identify the high potentials, and those employees get disproportionately more opportunities.

Is this a matter of Ivy Leaguers choosing the people most similar to them, or is it actually any kind of an indicator of performance that they'll do a better job?

I cannot tell you whether by personality or by ability they are better or worse leaders. One thing is for sure: throughout their careers they were affiliated with the right institutions—top universities but also top organizations. Where you studied and where you work can for the most part be a significant force in propelling you into the elite.

In the new career landscape, I don't think that this is going to be less important. In fact, it seems that it is going to be even more important than it is today.

I talked earlier about labor market institutions. Think about LinkedIn. LinkedIn allows hiring organizations to select on the basis of an individual's employer being a Fortune 100 or Fortune 500 company. Increasingly, more searches or job matches are done by LinkedIn. Professionals affiliated with the largest companies may therefore get even more visibility than they did in the pre-LinkedIn era.

What about headhunters?
Executive search firms in the new employment landscape are just as important as they were 15 years ago. Maybe they are even more important. My research shows that search firms also increasingly look for people affiliated with the most prestigious organizations. In my data set a couple of years ago, I analyzed the search data of an executive search firm. One-third of those executive candidates were working for the so-called elite corporations, corporations on the Fortune Most Admired list, for example. Thus, we have more evidence that elite affiliation will be even more important in the future, not less important.

Tell us about the CEO experience trap, which came out of some other research you carried out.
In this research we looked at CEOs of the Standard & Poor's 500 companies. About 20 percent of these executives have already had a CEO position with another corporation. In other words, they've had CEO experience. The research found that this past CEO experi-

ence, the job-specific experience, had hindered them in their current position. The title of our research that was published in the *MIT Sloan Management Review* is "The CEO Experience Trap," and from the title you can probably guess the result. We found that previous CEO experience actually doesn't help current performance at the helm of the organization. These CEOs actually performed worse than their counterparts who didn't have previous CEO experience.

We also tried to untangle why it may happen, and we pretty much had three theories. We approached this from three angles. First of all, we thought that experienced CEOs may perform worse in their new positions because they are taking over more troubled companies, in other words, companies that have a worse financial situation than the companies of the nonexperienced CEOs. But we found that this is not true. We don't find statistically significant differences in financial performance between these groups of companies.

Second, we thought that experienced CEOs may perform worse in the new organization because they are coming from the outside, whereas nonexperienced CEOs are often promoted internally. Again, though, this doesn't explain the worse performance of the experienced CEOs. Thus, we don't quite know what is going on, but our guess is that probably, in their new positions, these experienced CEOs are trying to use a recipe for decisions that they worked out in their previous positions. Because the context is different from that of the previous company, these old strategies no longer work. They actually hinder their performance in their current organizations. This is why it is called the CEO experience trap.

CHAPTER 5

Strategy Redux

"Deploy forces to defend the strategic points; exercise vigilance in preparation, do not be indolent," wrote Sun Tzu in *The Art of War*. "Deeply investigate the true situation, secretly await their laxity. Wait until they leave their strongholds, then seize what they love."[1] There is something reassuringly brutal about old-school strategy. It brooked no intervention. It was black and white, conquer or be conquered.

The trouble is that the world is increasingly gray and has always been complicated. For business leaders, the options are now global and decisions have to be taken in a fast-moving environment. What to do? The reality is that executives tend to have a particular approach or strategy that they repeat throughout their careers.

We spent time on a project with a senior executive who worked in three- or four-year cycles. He would get jobs—all with corporate marque names at a senior level—and go through the same process in each one. Then, as the results of his work began to trickle in, he would move on. He was successful, but his approach was formulaic, more of a well-appointed straitjacket than a strategy.

It is perhaps a cause for concern that over recent years the field of strategy has been somewhat neglected as academics and others have flocked to technology and innovation. This is misguided because in tumultuous times organizations still need strategies; indeed, they need them more than ever.

Build, Borrow, or Buy

Among those most successfully clarifying the power of strategy and the available options is Laurence Capron, the Paul Desmarais Chaired Professor of Partnership and Active Ownership at INSEAD in France. She is the coauthor, with Will Mitchell of Toronto University's Rotman School of Management, of *Build, Borrow, or Buy* (2012). Drawing on their research and teaching, Capron and Mitchell propose the Resource Pathways Framework, which is built around three strategic questions:

- **Build.** Are your existing internal resources relevant for developing internally the new resources that you have targeted for growth?
- **Borrow.** Could you obtain the targeted resources via an effective relationship with a resource partner through licensing or alliances?

- **Buy.** Do you need broad and deep relationships with your resource provider and need to take majority control?

We talked to Laurence Capron at INSEAD's Fontainebleau campus on the outskirts of Paris.

What first ignited your interest in this subject?

The starting point was my dissertation on mergers and acquisitions (M&As) and how they often destroy value. This was not only from a shareholder standpoint but also for employees, and M&As also could hurt a firm's capabilities. My initial interest was the extent to which acquisitions could help firms acquire new capabilities to continue to grow and survive and how often they ended up not being successful.

I started to develop executive programs on M&As at INSEAD. It became clear to me that executives—heads of M&As, corporate development, and so on—came to the course with the idea that M&As *were* the strategy of their company and they just needed to make it happen. Instead of being a tool in a tool kit, M&As were the strategy. The executives tended not to think whether they needed M&As in the first place to accomplish what they needed to accomplish; when it makes sense to make an M&A; or whether there are alternatives: What about a joint venture, a licensing agreement, internal development, or corporate entrepreneurship?

Part of the course increasingly became about when not to make an acquisition and the alternative tools. Then of course the question became: When should I make an acquisition instead of using other tools?

Then, following the likes of Penrose, Prahalad, and Hamel, I tried to better understand how a firm can grow its set of resources and really deploy them successfully. I was strongly attracted to that resource-based stream of research. I found it extremely insightful to look at a corporation as a set of core resources. I really liked the idea in C. K. Prahalad's initial work of these resources being trapped in their business unit and how even corporations had difficulties in accessing their own resources, their internal innovation, and their ability to move resources around.

There have been lots of questions raised about M&As for a long time, about them destroying value rather than building it and about the egos involved and people being blind to other opportunities. It's amazing that companies' enthusiasm for M&As persists.

If you look at the entire process from due diligence, assessment, portfolio fit, pricing, postmerger integration, and then potentially learning and codification and putting in good templates, we all know that through the process it's very easy to stumble. What has been more interesting for me as I've developed cases on companies such as Cisco and Monsanto, among others, is that even good acquirers can stumble. They have developed M&A best practice, but at some point the organization becomes geared toward making acquisitions again and again, to some extent losing sight of the role of internal innovation, how important it is to build organic growth as well as acquiring businesses, and how they should balance alliances, acquisitions, and organic growth.

I really do believe—and it's the key thesis developed in *Build, Borrow, or Buy*, which I wrote with Will Mitchell—that firms that select their growth modes on the basis of the circumstances they face tend to perform better and survive in comparison with firms that specialize in one mode.

What it means is that even if you are an M&A specialist, a firm that becomes extremely good at making acquisition deals and relies on that acquisition growth, at some point you will hit the wall and have to step back to stop, to sequence, and to build back organic growth or access new capabilities through licensing or alliances. Not every valuable external partner wants to be bought. They may instead want to engage in a flexible collaborative agreement. Again, to access the different valuable sources of innovation, it's really important to tap into the different modes.

Isn't the trouble that the build and borrow options are quite dull, whereas buying is exciting?

Yes, buying is exciting; we know that. Therefore, for a CEO it's very tempting to go for buying. We know that firms and their leaders need strong corporate discipline to keep their hubris in check and avoid being carried away in the M&A process. Even value-creating

M&As need to be complemented with internal innovation and over time must blend effectively internal
skills and talents with those of external people.

But the importance of balance is a difficult message,
isn't it?
Yes, it's very difficult because usually CEOs and the
top management teams don't question their mode
of growth. If you have always grown with a specific
mode and have been rather successful, you just go
on. If firms are successful with their first acquisitions,
they keep going without assessing that at some point
they are going to run out of integration skills and their
people are going to be tired of screening, buying, and
integrating new firms.

   This balance is very important. Again, it's very
difficult—not at an intellectual level because the
build, borrow, buy framework is very simple but at a
behavioral, political, and emotional level—for firms to
consider all their options on an equal footing. CEOs,
for instance, if they have an engineering background,
will tend to emphasize the engineering part and internal innovation; if they come more from a financial
background, they will focus more on deal making as a
solution. Background is very important.

   There are also pressures. CEOs and top management teams suffer from internal and external pressures
when it comes to making deals. It's very difficult in
terms of behavior to consider the different options
you have.

What we still see in organizations is that the different functions tend to be located at different levels. For instance, the M&A team is usually very close to the CEO and the corporate development team, but the licensing team or the alliance team tends to be folded at a much lower level within the organization. It's really up to the CEO to consider all these options equally, to have the discipline to say when it makes sense to make an alliance rather than going through a potentially value-destroying acquisition.

Are you saying that if they're interested in longer-term stability and development of the company, they need to seek out balance?

Yes. The short-term pressures are in favor of pursuing instinctive implementation excellence of a favorite mode of growth—what we call the implementation trap—instead of reviewing the alternative modes of growth options available in light of the company's knowledge base and values, the nature of the targeted resources, the resource market characteristics, and the nature of the desired relationship with an external partner. Often companies specialize in one mode ("one-trick ponies") for short-term efficiency, but long term, when you look at it, companies go through cycles of build, borrow, buy more defensively than proactively.

If we think of firms such as Nokia, BlackBerry, and Dell, we know that all firms at some point face a tension between exploration and exploitation: exploiting the core versus exploring and stretching the core.

It's very easy when you think of exploration to jump on acquisitions as the solution to your problems. When their core business is under threat, companies tend to keep on investing in R&D, because it's hard to cut back R&D programs; to restructure internally; and, at the same time, to embark on a series of unrelated acquisitions. As a result, they end up with a very fragmented portfolio of projects. What you have are very contradictory pressures.

Where does a company such as Apple fit into the build, borrow, or buy framework?
What is interesting with Apple is that they started focusing on internal innovation. They're very proud of their products and their internal culture. The company was driven by innovation, and the culture was all about great products and being proud of them. What is amazing about Apple, in spite of its strong preference for internal innovation, is that it managed to build a strong network of outside partners and combined that with focused educational acquisitions in domains such as computer software, mobile advertising, and mapping services; usually these have not been very visible because they're not big transformational acquisitions. Apple has been very good at combining the three elements.

Who else does this well, do you think?
We have Cisco as an example in the book. Cisco became an M&A machine in the late 1990s. But after

70 acquisitions, it ran out of integration skills, people were demotivated, and so on. Cisco completely restructured to put more weight on intrapreneurship and to balance the three modes. If you look at Cisco in terms of corporate strategy, it has alliances, acquisitions, and intrapreneurship.

Or look at L'Oréal. Out of its 28 major brands 25 were acquired. But what is really interesting about L'Oréal is that it managed to build organic growth once it acquired those companies.

Does the framework work globally?

Of course, in some parts of the world, such as the Middle East, alliances between business groups and families are more important than the buy mode. It depends how developed the market for corporate control is. If you are in the Boston area, where there is a strong market for VCs, for collaborations between start-ups and incumbents, and so on, it might be easier to trade IP and to go for contractual arrangements first.

Also, there are some regulatory barriers. For entry into some markets you may need to have a local partner. Those are the contextual factors that will influence the framework.

No matter where you are, the starting point is our assumption that CEOs have clarified their strategy. The gap we try to close is really about the selection and the balance of the mode.

In your experience, do CEOs have a strategy?

I hope so! They can be driven by opportunities and so on, but at big companies they have processes in place to review their strategy. Therefore, at least we know that companies are equipped with strategic planning processes. Do they follow them closely? It's case by case.

We found that when CEOs have clarified where they want to go and the activity they need to survive, usually they jump to their favorite mode. What we tried to accomplish in the build, borrow, buy framework is this idea of stepping back and saying that before you jump to your favorite mode, whether it's internal or alliances or acquisition, make sure to think carefully about the best way to grow and avoid the main traps.

What are the main traps you found?

The first is in most cases that there is a strong preference for internal development. Thus, companies will usually first try experimenting internally, and it's only once they have failed that they go externally. But if the gap is too big, the organization is not appropriate to develop what you need and you should go externally much more quickly.

The second trap is that once companies have figured that internal development is not fast enough or appropriate and have decided to look externally, instead of considering the full range of external options—from licensing to alliances to JVs [joint ventures] and so on—they jump to acquisition. They think they have already wasted too much time and jump to acquisitions with the idea that acquisitions are a quick fix, a shortcut.

Another misleading assumption is that if you get full control, you will get full access to the capabilities. Mostly it's not true. People walk away, and full control doesn't necessarily give you easy access to capabilities. In the study we did on 162 telecom firms, 27 percent of the acquiring firms managed to extract the value of the target's firm capabilities and 80 percent chose acquisitions over alliances to get exclusive access to the targeted capabilities. Access to external capabilities hinges on the willingness of people to collaborate. By creating a trauma, full control through M&As can in fact be an impediment to collaborative behavior.

The third trap is not considering postacquisition issues, particularly the motivation of people.

Where does this research lead to now?

Now I'm working on applying build, borrow, buy to young companies. With a colleague in the United States, Asli Arikan, I am tracking the population of firms that went for an IPO [initial public offering]. We're looking at about 4,000 firms and what happened to them and their likelihood of delisting. It's interesting because by the end of the fifth year after an IPO, 55 percent of firms are delisted. We are trying to reexamine the relationship between the type of corporate development programs they have been following and their likelihood of being delisted.

We are finding that young companies that do too many acquisitions or too many alliances in the five years after their IPOs are more likely to be delisted. Most likely they run out of resources to integrate properly what they buy.

But we also find that firms that stick with internal development are also more likely to be delisted. Thus, if you rely only on internal development, that can also penalize a young IPO firm. Similarly, a young IPO firm needs to find the optimal path between relying too much on internal development, which most likely is going to be too slow for it to scale up its organization and speed up its innovation, and having too much openness, too many acquisitions that can also hurt the firm because it doesn't have the competency and skills to embark on such an aggressive program just after an IPO. Most of them when they go IPO don't have acquisition experience; they tend to be young with little corporate development function.

Thus, young firms still need to engage in affiliation, partnership, and maybe some focused acquisition in addition to their internal development.

With a doctoral student from INSEAD, Aline Gatignon, we are examining how domestic firms in Brazil that are not affiliated to a business group develop leading-edge capabilities, with the prominent role of the borrow mode reflected in the cross-sector multilateral alliances forged among key players in the ecosystem.

What about the field of strategy generally? When you first entered that field in the 1990s, there were lots of interesting people involved in strategy. Now it seems slightly unfashionable.

Yes. I see two different environments. In the practitioner environment interest in strategy and corporate development is huge. When it comes to M&As, alliances, and corporate development, these topics are important for every firm, because firms face digitalization, want to be more socially conscious, and so on. Achieving a competitive advantage is still the core of practitioners' interest.

The academic market is structured around publications, and there is a shortage of scholars in what we call pure strategy. To some extent in the academic environment people want to be embedded in a discipline such as sociology or economics. The business education market asks for more relevance. A school such as INSEAD has to try to live with those kinds of contradictory forces, providing relevant teaching and research for the different stakeholders but also paying attention to rigor and remaining open to different streams of research, including the discipline-based type of approach.

CHAPTER 6

Innovation Now

Historically, innovation has tended to take place in two stereotypical locations. The first is Silicon Valley, with its high-tech start-ups: big ideas, high fives, world-changing ambitions, and so on. The more traditional home of innovation is the corporate R&D center: techies, wisdom, and knowledge condensed into a single building crammed full with bright ideas.

No more. Recent years have seen an assault on those innovation standards. Innovation is not a function of wacky creativity or the size of the R&D budget. To mix our metaphors, it is increasingly difficult to pigeonhole or keep a lid on innovation. Bright ideas are suddenly everywhere. But how do you find the right ones?

The Field of Thinkers

Amid the crowded innovation field, we have identified a handful of people whose work stands out as original. Worth watching are the following:

- **Ron Adner.** Professor of strategy at the Tuck School at Dartmouth College in New Hampshire, Adner is the author of *The Wide Lens: A New Strategy for Innovation* (2012), which has been heralded as a pathbreaking guide to successful innovation in an interdependent world. He is also the author of the *Harvard Business Review* article "Match Your Innovation Strategy to Your Innovation Ecosystem."
- **Erik Brynjolfsson.** The Schussel Family Professor of Management at the MIT Sloan School of Management, the director of the MIT Center for Digital Business, and a research associate at the National Bureau of Economic Research, Brynjolfsson focuses on how businesses can effectively use information technology. He is the co-author, with Andrew McAfee, of *Race Against the Machine* (2012).
- **Prasad Kaipa.** The coauthor with Navi Radjou of *From Smart to Wise: Acting and Leading with Wisdom* (2013), Kaipa has gone in his work from research and teaching in physics at the University of Utah, to international marketing at Apple, to teaching in executive education. Along the way, he founded SelfCorp and cofounded an entrepreneur institute for TiE (The Indus Entrepreneurs) in 2002. In 2003, he started working

with the Indian School of Business in Hyderabad, focusing most recently on wise leadership, affordable or frugal innovation, and cross-cultural models of leadership, change, and innovation.

- **Max Wessel.** A fellow at Harvard Business School's Forum for Growth and Innovation, a think tank devoted to developing academic understanding of the innovation process, Wessel has conducted research focused on product development, how companies can adapt to changing market conditions, and identifying the technologies that enable disruption. He is coauthoring a book on product design, innovation, and new product marketing with Clayton M. Christensen and Scott D. Anthony. He advises various venture-backed start-ups in the consumer Internet and clean tech industries and has founded a consumer Internet company. He has a BA in economics and philosophy from Northwestern University and an MBA from Harvard Business School.

Scaling Innovation

A fellow at the Forum for Growth and Innovation at Harvard Business School, James Allworth has an MBA from Harvard and previously worked for Apple and Booz and Co. His work focuses on technology and disruption. He is a regular contributor to the *Harvard Business Review* and coauthor of the bestseller *How Will You Measure Your Life?* (with Clay Christensen and Karen Dillon, 2012).

Now Allworth is based in Palo Alto and is the director of strategy at the late-stage start-up Medallia.

How do you explain what you do and who you are?
You're not easy to categorize.

No, and on some level I like that about myself. If there's a common thread that runs through everything I've done, it's that I've pursued things that I'm interested in. It's never necessarily been an industry focus or an academic versus professional focus or anything like that. I've been really lucky to have had opportunities to go out and do interesting things, and whenever an interesting problem or an interesting opportunity presents itself, I really can't help myself. It doesn't matter what it is. If I think it's interesting, I'll jump on it.

Does that link your work at Booz, Apple, and at Harvard?

Yes, coming out of undergraduate studies, I, like a lot of people, didn't entirely know what I was getting myself into but consider myself very fortunate to have landed in management consulting; it's a great grounding for thinking about big business problems. I also had a number of very rough edges that I had ground off while I was in consulting, did some really interesting work, strategy and operations, throughout Australia and Southeast Asia, and got to live in Thailand for a year and in Indonesia for six months.

After business school, I got some time at Apple, which was fantastic, working in their retail team looking at how they sell to business customers, and then got an opportunity to work with Clay Christensen, which was really never part of the plan.

Why did you go to business school in the first place?
What was the attraction?

Intellectual curiosity and stimulation. I visited Harvard before I was accepted, and you just get that sense from wandering around the campus and visiting their classrooms and seeing people talk in between classes and what they're talking about. Environments like that are magnetizing.

Tell us about the class by Clay Christensen that proved important.

The class is called "Building and Sustaining a Successful Enterprise." It's one of the most popular elective classes, and the basic idea is that every class you come in and learn about a new theory, and then you discuss the theory in the context of the case. It is slightly different from most of the other classes at HBS in that most of them are primarily focused on the cases. This is different in that you focus on the theory, and the case is there only as an opportunity to ground the theory and have a discussion about it.

How did you make the leap from the classroom to becoming a coauthor?

Clay and I got along really well, and I don't know if it was in part because of my Australian heritage or perhaps because I was slightly ignorant and would always stick my hand up and ask difficult questions. I imagine a number of professors wouldn't like that, but Clay absolutely loved it. He asked me whether I'd be interested in sticking around for a little while and working with him afterward.

What did you learn in the process of writing the book How Will You Measure Your Life? *with Clay and Karen Dillon?*

I learned a lot. When Clay talked to me about doing this and I agreed, we didn't actually know what it was that I was going to be doing; the book kind of emerged. Karen and Clay worked together on the article that was in the *Harvard Business Review* that bears the same title. Clay and I were talking about working on something more marketing-related, and a week after I started he had a stroke.

We're very fortunate that he made a full recovery, but events like that cause you to stop and think about life. I found myself drawing on Clay's last class, where he takes all the theories and writes them up on the board and then writes three questions beside them: How can I find happiness in my relationships? How can I find happiness in my career? How can I stay out of jail?

From my perspective, I certainly don't have all the answers, and part of what I really like about the way Clay approaches problems in general is that he doesn't think he does either, but he has a knack for asking great questions and he's also got an amazing ability to look at research and see whether it's causal in nature. That means that when you apply it to different fields, you're able to get deep insight into the questions you're asking.

Part of the appeal of working on the book was that it was not just an opportunity to share this thinking but also an opportunity for me to think about it in the context of my own life, and yes, applying the theories and writing about them and spending the time with Clay and Karen working on them and pushing our thinking forward was immensely valuable.

Twenty years ago it was very easy for us to say these are the strategy guys, these are the innovation guys, these are the entrepreneurial guys, but you can't do that now. People such as yourself seem to defy categorization.

This reflects something I believe in: the most interesting things happen on the boundaries where you find intersections between various fields. What drives me in terms of what I apply myself to, what I write about, is literally nothing more than things that I'm interested in and things that I become passionate about. When you focus on things like that, it becomes easy to do a really good job, to write things that people deeply engage with, to build ideas that end up having an outsized impact. I'm naturally a bit of a generalist, and I think there's value in being like that.

Even so, it's a big leap from Harvard to Palo Alto.
Less so than you might think, actually.

Tell us about the ideas you are currently working on.
One of the things I've become really fascinated with is the intersection between motivation and organizational structures. Now, if you think about the world 50 years ago, it was very much set up to optimize organizations to ensure that they were able to control the largest number of resources possible. Scale was critical to winning, whether in the military or in business.

If you think about the way the world has changed, in part as a result of technology, scale is not necessarily such an advantage anymore. Rather than the organizations that are able to command and control the most people being the ones that end up winning, it ends up being organizations that are able to attract the best people and get the best out of them.

What's interesting about this is that organizational structures have not really adapted to this new world. There's a lot of scope to improve the way organizations are designed to get the best out of the people who are working in them.

There's one example that people like to talk about that really illustrates this well, and that's Valve Software, a gaming company based in Washington State. When people are hired at Valve, they are given a desk with wheels. Nobody is able to tell anybody else what to do, there's no boss, there's no hierarchy, and you're literally able to do whatever you want. What's interesting is that it really taps into people's motivations. People no longer do things because they have been told what to do or feel they have to do them. They start to do things because of intrinsic motivation; they become passionate about the project, opt into it, or come up with an idea and sell other people in the organization on the project and get other people excited about it. Then they drive it through to completion based on that intrinsic satisfaction from getting something done, doing something great, getting it out the door.

It's something that I want to explore further. It's really interesting in the context of how technology has enabled fewer and fewer people to have a greater and greater impact on the world, but the way organizations are designed has not evolved, with very few exceptions, to recognize that change.

But isn't there a sense that it's the ambiguity people can't cope with or are uncomfortable with historically? The types of problems that people in organizations are getting outsized rewards for tackling are the ambiguous ones for which there aren't clear answers. The people best suited to attacking those problems are comfortable with ambiguity. They're attracted to ambiguous, loosely defined, and hard to solve problems and need to have an organizational structure that is helpful rather than a hindrance to them.

You have worked in two of the most stratified and organizationally traditional industries: management consulting and academia.
Yes. I mean I have, so you'll get no argument from me about the fact that management consulting is very

stratified, at least in terms of titles, but on the teams I've worked with it always felt incredibly flat. There was never an instance when I felt like my role was to be seen and not heard; it was an environment in which people were encouraged to speak up.

Now, academia is similar, but one of the things I observed in working with Clay is that he absolutely trusts everyone he works with to do the right thing. His question is not, When are you going to get this done? His question is always, What can I do to help you be effective?

You know, when people take that attitude with you, they empower you, and that really tends to bring out the best in people.

You talked about scale as well. Is the nature of scale changing?

Yes. I have a colleague from the Forum for Growth and Innovation, Max Wessel, and he's converted me to the idea that scale is becoming commoditized.

For example, if you wanted to set up a web company 10 years ago, you needed to buy servers, get storage, and set it all up yourself. But all that capex [capital expenditure] has been turned into opex [operational expenditure].

There are always organizations such as Apple that have to do it themselves because they're pushing the boundaries, but for a lot of organizations scale is available to be bought. You don't have to get on the

ground in China, build your own factories, and do all
these kinds of things.

The traditional version of scale has been commoditized, but what's replacing it?

*To what extent are you putting your ideas into practice
at Medallia?*
There is always a balance between thinking and doing.
I definitely think, though, that the extent to which I've
been lucky enough to be exposed to and have a good
understanding of Clay's research is really helpful. He
informs a lot of the discussions I have with people,
and I'm able to use it to inform the projects that I'm
undertaking as well. I don't think it would be possible
for me to go into work every day and not rely on that
research and those theories to a greater or lesser extent.

*One of your other interests that is intriguing is the rise
of autonomous vehicles.*
This is very much further afield: How is the world
going to start to change as a result of autonomous
vehicles: drones and self-driving vehicles? I think that's
going to prompt an absolutely massive shift, and there
are a number of really interesting companies out here
doing things relating to this. I've been able to meet a
few of them, and just thinking about how the world's
going to change as a result is absolutely fascinating.

What's going to be very interesting to see is what
happens to a lot of the vehicle manufacturers as these

self-driving vehicles get to the point where they're ready to be deployed. We live in a world where when someone wants a car, he or she goes out and buys one, and the utilization rates run at 10 percent or less. Most of the vehicle's life is spent parked. If these self-driving vehicles take off, thinking how the world changes as a result is absolutely fascinating. Utilization rates go up.

Personal transport then begins to look a lot more like the airline industry, where you have a few manufacturers, than it does at present. Effectively, the vehicles become commoditized and there are likely to be only a few manufacturers left. People don't really care whether they fly in a Boeing or an Airbus plane anymore, and it's going to be the same in the future with vehicles.

The question then becomes who is well placed to take advantage. This is where I wonder whether a UPS or a FedEx is actually well positioned. They're used to deploying lots of capital to move things around. Right now it's parcels, but I wonder how much of a stretch it would be to change that to humans. The other organization I wonder about is Uber. Now they're just a car service, but they're also generating vast quantities of data around daily movement patterns, weekly movement patterns, monthly movement patterns, where vehicles are needed, where people ride to and from. They announced something around financing cars, and I wonder whether this isn't a step toward thinking further down the line of owning a fleet of autonomous vehicles. It sounds like science fiction, but that's the direction where we're heading and it's really interesting to play out the impacts of that, how the world looks so different.

What about Silicon Valley? Has that been energizing?
Absolutely. I mean, there's just so many cool people out here doing so much cool stuff that it's impossible to stay on top of it all. I'm living a couple of blocks away from Stanford, and there are always interesting things happening there, seminars and so on; you get to meet some fascinating people working on fascinating projects. It really feels to me like this place is changing the world right now, and listening and hearing more about all the things that people are doing and getting to play a small part in that has been really fantastic.

There's no plan for the future?
Well, the plan remains, as it always has been, as long as things are interesting and I remain passionate about what I'm doing, I'm learning new things, and I'm working with great people, the plan remains to keep doing that. Right now I'm very, very lucky to be at Medallia doing exactly that, and I hope it continues.

By Jugaad

New inspirations for innovation come from unexpected places. Take what is called jugaad innovation and its key promoter, Navi Radjou. A fellow at Cambridge Judge Business School, where he is the former executive director of the Centre for India & Global Business, Radjou is the coauthor (with Jaideep Prabhu and

Simone Ahuja) of *Jugaad Innovation: Think Frugal, Be Flexible, Generate Breakthrough Growth* (Jossey-Bass, 2012) and (with Prasad Kaipa) *From Smart to Wise* (Jossey-Bass, 2013). He won the 2013 Thinkers50 India Innovation Award as well as the 2013 Thinkers50 Innovation Award.

Can you explain the big idea behind jugaad innovation?
The idea behind jugaad innovation is to provide an alternative to the traditional model of innovation that is prevalent in the West. If you look at the approach to innovation in developed economies such as the United States, Europe, and Japan, for the past 50-plus years the formula has been pretty much standardized. Essentially, it is a big R&D budget and fancy R&D labs. It takes many, many months and sometimes years to come up with what researchers believe are awesome products. But many of them flop in the marketplace.

Just because you invest in big costly R&D projects, that doesn't make you innovative, let alone successful. This became even more important after the economic crisis that began in 2008, when companies were cash-strapped. That's when we began to look at a different model of innovation that will continue to help companies come up with new products and services but will be more affordable and more sustainable as well.

We ended up looking at the emerging markets as an inspiration for this new model of innovation. In particular, we looked at India, where the economy is very complex and there is widespread scarcity of resources. What we discovered is that even though there is a lot of resource scarcity in those emerging markets, people are resourceful. They tap into something that is abundant within themselves: their ingenuity. Jugaad in a nutshell is that resilient ingenuity that people tap into to come up with very frugal products and services that deliver greater value for their fellow citizens at lower costs. These frugal solutions include a fridge made entirely of clay that consumes no electricity, a low-cost portable infant warmer for premature babies, a mobile service that lets you send and receive money without having a bank account, and an advertising billboard that converts air humidity into drinkable water. The list goes on and on.

This is a new approach to innovation that we think is very frugal, very sustainable. It is also very agile because you get products and services out very quickly, and it's also inclusive because you can bring value to a broader segment of the community, many of whom might be traditionally marginalized in the economy.

Where does the expression jugaad come from?

Jugaad is a word from Punjabi, one of the many Indian languages. Literally, it describes a makeshift vehicle built by villagers using whatever parts they can find. It's like a Frankenstein kind of thing in which the back of the vehicle is a bullock cart and at the front there is a tractor engine. It's a way of transporting people from villages to cities whenever they have to go to cities. It is basically an ad hoc vehicle made up of spare parts cobbled together.

Jugaad, then, is the ability to not reinvent the wheel all the time but to see what you already have around you and then make the most of it.

Is there an equivalent phrase in English?
Do it yourself, or DIY, is probably the closest English expression. In social sciences there is a famous term that was introduced by Claude Lévi-Strauss, the famous French anthropologist, in the 1960s. He called it *bricolage*, and the term has recently been picked up in several Western business schools and used as an ad hoc translation or an equivalent to "resourceful improvisation." DIY or *bricolage* would be a Western term for this notion of jugaad. The growing Maker Movement in the West embodies this resourceful DIY spirit.

Jugaad is a great term and the timing was perfect in terms of what was going on with the world's economy, but how did you actually identify organizations doing this and find out how they were doing it?
It was a very interesting coincidence or confluence of different factors and people coming together. In my case, I started my career in the United States in the late 1990s as an analyst at Forrester Research helping Western companies become more innovative. In the early 2000s I began to pay attention to what was happening in India, particularly the innovative services offered by IT [information technology] service companies such as Tata Consultancy Services and Infosys.

As a regular visitor to India, I started interacting with dozens of innovative entrepreneurs and corporations there during each visit.

That was when I connected with the Tata Group, which at that time was beginning to develop the $2,000 Nano car. To be candid, initially I didn't view the Nano as an innovation because of the dominant Western innovation model in which I was trained. I had studied in France, a country famous for its scientific, R&D-driven innovation, and everything I knew about innovation was challenged in emerging markets such as India where I saw people with very few resources who were able to come up with a lot of clever solutions such as the Nano.

Initially I dismissed the Indian approach and solutions such as the Nano as low-cost stuff that couldn't qualify as innovation, but then I began to rethink what innovation really means. I realized that what matters with any innovation is that it actually creates more value for people. That's really the point, and from that perspective, a lot of the frugal solutions that are developed in India and other emerging markets do bring a lot of value for the local community.

That was when I realized the need to formalize this frugal and flexible approach to innovation because one of the challenges in emerging markets is that there is a lot of untapped tacit knowledge. They have been doing jugaad for centuries, if not millennia, so they don't really see what's so interesting about it that is worth studying and sharing with the rest of the world.

But for me, as a researcher with a global outlook, I was very excited and thought this was exactly the doctor's prescription for our resource-constrained world.

As I began to study the jugaad phenomenon, I joined Cambridge University in 2009 to launch the Centre for India & Global Business with Professor Jaideep Prabhu at Judge Business School. The Centre gave us a platform to rigorously study the new innovation models and practices in emerging markets and bring them to the Western world. Jaideep became my partner in crime in this journey. We were soon joined by the third protagonist, Dr. Simone Ahuja. Simone was a film producer, and she was making a documentary on grassroots innovation in Indian villages. I was an advisor for her film. That's how the three of us connected.

We ended up forming a nice triad. With my consulting background, I brought in practical experience, Simone brought in great right brain capabilities like storytelling and design sensibility, and Jaideep brought in academic rigor. That's how we combined these individual qualities to co-create our book *Jugaad Innovation*.

Sounds like a dream team. What you were describing with jugaad innovation was typical of the way some people in the community and small Indian companies work. But were you also seeing this approach with large companies such as Tata? Did they use a more jugaad approach than Western companies do?

That's correct. Jugaad is more of a mindset than a methodology, and that frugal and flexible mindset is prevalent and is manifested across companies of all sectors and all sizes. It is used by not-for-profit as well as for-profit companies, grassroots entrepreneurs in the tiniest villages, all the way to big corporations such as Tata Group and subsidiaries of multinational companies such as Siemens and Unilever operating in emerging markets such as India.

Is this primarily an Indian thing, or do you see it in other emerging economies? Is it something that would work in the West?

We will come to the West in a minute, but jugaad is definitely practiced in many other emerging markets. Africa and Brazil particularly are the closest, and China as well. In Africa, they call it *kanju*, and in Brazil it's called *gambiarra*. The Chinese call it *jiejian chuangxin* ("frugal innovation"). China is often accused of copying Western innovation, but there is now a big push by the Chinese government to come up with indigenous innovation inspired by local needs that creates greater value at a low cost for Chinese citizens.

Jugaad is also quite prevalent in China in terms of how local entrepreneurs and companies can quickly come up with new products and services by being very frugal and agile in the way they develop solutions. Similarly, in Africa you see a lot of jugaad kinds of approaches, such as using a bicycle to recharge your cell phone. What's fascinating is that more and more multinationals are now radically changing the way they innovate in emerging markets such as Africa by adopting this kind of jugaad mindset.

Can you give an example?
My favorite example is IBM. Researchers in the brand-new IBM lab in Nairobi, Kenya, are doing something fascinating that for me is really jugaad. It is a combination of low tech and high tech. They are taking in data feed from low-resolution webcams that track the traffic conditions in Nairobi streets and then analyzing that data by using high-end software algorithms to predict traffic jams and optimize traffic management. For me that's a fantastic example of jugaad innovation because you take what you have, which is these low-resolution webcams, and rather than upgrading them, which is expensive, you start with that and you say this is all we have, and then what can I add on top of that, which is these software algorithms, which are developed cost-effectively by IBM's army of programmers.

That combination is creating an amazing solution that is much more affordable for Kenyans than if they had to go for a very high-tech solution.

In the West, of course, we see jugaad taking off thanks to this whole Maker Movement with the 3D printing and the technology-led DIY philosophy of creating and reusing the objects we own. My hunch is that the jugaad revolution in the West might be more technology-enabled. Whereas in an emerging market jugaad is a bit more of a low-tech kind of movement, in the West it might be fueled by these emerging DIY technologies such as 3D printing, which is becoming democratized and more affordable.

As these DIY technologies become more widespread and become integrated with social networking tools, they will provide a platform for everyday citizens to unleash their ingenuity in a collaborative way. In both emerging markets and the West, however, the philosophy of jugaad is the same. It's all about tapping into one's ingenuity to improvise creative solutions, except that the tools might be a bit more high tech in the West than in emerging markets.

To some extent perhaps we are already seeing this with apps, because apps platforms, whether it's Apple or others, provide a high-tech platform that allows small developers to use their ingenuity to develop apps at a low cost.

Yes, that's already happening. Smartphones are becoming the new platform for "maker" entrepreneurs to develop affordable hardware solutions. Take CellScope, a start-up that is a spin-off of Berkeley University in California. CellScope has created accessories that you can attach to your iPhone and convert your smartphone into an otoscope or dermascope. If your kid is complaining of some ear problem, you just plug it in the ear and see if there is an ear infection. You don't have to go to the hospital, so it saves you time, and that attachment costs a fraction of even the lowest-end device used by a physician. In coming years, I see smartphones becoming a cost-effective hardware platform for developing all kinds of very affordable solutions in industries, such as healthcare, that need them the most.

Very exciting. What are the takeaways for managers? Are there lessons that can be imported back into the big multinationals, the big national companies?

First, I think we need to bring back the principle of KISS: keep it simple, stupid. In the West we have a tendency to make things complex. Our current R&D philosophy is, Why make things simpler when you can make them more complex? The first lesson is that we have to move away from what I call a just-in-case engineering mindset to a just-in-time engineering approach that yields good-enough solutions. Let me explain what I mean by that. It has been reported that many features in Microsoft Office applications are never used. Microsoft engineers overloaded Office with features just in case users would need them some day—but they never did! Instead of creating a good-enough solution with the features that users need the most, Microsoft ended up producing this monster Office software that is too bloated, expensive, and complex to use. They need to switch to a just-in-time design approach by asking: What is the strict minimum set of features that users really need so that they can immediately get the most value from the software? Then you focus on delivering just that, and later you can incrementally add more features to the software as required.

Can you give us an example of that?

Salesforce.com is a great practitioner of this just-in-time design approach: they dynamically add (or remove) features on the basis of massive real-time customer input. The lesson in that regard is: don't initially launch a too-complex overkill solution because you are going to alienate a lot of users. Start with something simple, frugal, or good enough, as we call it, and then iteratively improve it. That's one key lesson.

Other takeaways?

The second lesson is partner, partner, partner. I think one reason companies in emerging markets are so good at innovating faster and cheaper is that they rely heavily on third parties. They go deep into local communities and co-create solutions with many local partners. Large Western companies think they can do everything in-house.

I would say open up and engage suppliers, your local community, as co-creators rather than trying it on your own.

And the third lesson?

The third message with the jugaad mindset is around leadership. Leaders need to create space and time for employees to innovate—a playground where they can play. Google does that well. Jugaad, for me, has a childlike magic in it. Remember that *ingenious* sounds like *ingenuous*, which implies innocence and a sense of wonderment.

Employees are able to come up with the most innovative solutions when they are not encumbered by the rigid processes and structures of companies. Large companies are too uptight right now, and the only way they can loosen up is by converting the workplace into a playground. One company that has done this very well is Ford. They have partnered in Detroit with TechShop, which provides a maker platform, to repurpose a warehouse as a big playground where Ford employees can go in their spare time—evenings and weekends—and toy with 3D printers and other DIY technologies without any constraints. It's a playground where they can do whatever creative projects they want.

Through that process, the Ford engineers are able to come up with really innovative ideas that otherwise they would not do inside a formal R&D lab where there are more restrictions. Thanks to this initiative, Ford has managed to increase the amount of patentable ideas by 50 percent while reducing its R&D spending by a significant percentage. Literally, they can now innovate much more with a lot less.

That for me is the third big takeaway: jugaad happens only in a very messy environment. The more processes you put in and the more structured the environment is, the more innovation becomes very incremental. People take only small steps and keep watching their backs. But when employees are given freedom to think and act like kids in a playground, they don't give a damn about rules; they just go and play and try to break the rules. That's how you get disruptive innovation.

Innovation has become too serious in corporations. We need to rekindle its playful side. Companies need to bring back the magic and fun element of innovation.

What are you working on now? What should we be looking at in your direction?

I'm very excited because I'm working on two big projects in 2014 that are both related to jugaad. First, I am curating a big exhibition sponsored by a large European firm. It is an exhibition that will celebrate human ingenuity in its purest form. We will show how in the developed as well as the developing world everyday citizens, entrepreneurs, and visionary companies are innovating in a frugal, flexible, and inclusive manner to come up with affordable and sustainable solutions that address the most pressing needs in our societies. This exhibition will be launched in Paris in late 2014 and then will travel all around the world.

I'm very happy to bring this kind of optimistic message to the masses so that they can be inspired to use their own ingenuity to solve pressing problems in their local communities.

The second big project I'm working on is a book on frugal innovation, a sequel to *Jugaad Innovation*, but this time focusing more on the developed world. This new book will show how even wealthy economies—such as the United States, Europe, Japan, South Korea, Singapore, and Australia—are adopting frugal innovation to address the needs of cost-conscious and environmentally active citizens.

We have some very, very cool case studies of companies doing frugal innovation, especially in France and Europe, and that's something that baffles me. I have spent the last 15 years in the United States and have seen a lot of the big ideas in the past coming from here, like open innovation. P&G is an American company that pioneered open innovation in 2000. But interestingly, this time around I feel Europe is way ahead of the United States in the practice of frugal innovation. That's exciting for me because I am a French national and have been collecting amazing case studies on European pioneers of frugal innovation, whether it's Pearson, Unilever, Siemens, or Renault-Nissan; the list goes on and on. I am really perplexed to not have found yet any large U.S. company really doing frugal innovation, although there is a growing number of entrepreneurs in America who are doing it.

That worries me because I admire American companies and have always viewed the U.S. economy as a global trendsetter. But lately I worry that U.S. companies are not thinking big enough. I feel they have become a bit too complacent. If so, they have to be careful because they may be missing out on frugal innovation, which is a megatrend that is starting to emerge. U.S. companies, especially U.S. multinationals, have to look at what's happening not only in dynamic emerging markets such as India and Africa but also in what they call Old Europe, which I believe is finally reawakening.

Sustaining the Future

The big issues of the world are impinging on the boardroom and the corporate suite as never before. Companies are at the front line in tackling global warming and much more. Corporate social responsibility (CSR) has moved from an often decorative adornment to a central activity for many organizations.

The ability of academics to keep up to date with the changing shape of organizations and with evolving executive priorities has long been questioned. Post hoc analysis and rationalization is the order of the academic day. How do and should academics deal with issues such as sustainability and CSR? Should they leave them to play out and then provide analysis? Among those advocating and practicing a more interventionist approach is Ioannis Ioannou of London Business School.

"A number of critical global trends, including the rising acute scarcity of natural resources, climate change, and massive demographic changes around the world, combined with increasing levels of income inequality and an unprecedented shift of middle-class consumption from the developed to the developing world, are radically shifting the world's competitive landscape," says Ioannou. "The winning sustainable organizations of the future will be the ones that acknowledge these tectonic shifts today and are able to strategically and uniquely integrate such broader social and environmental issues into their business models, their corporate cultures, and their strategies. They are the organizations that will be able to synergistically cogenerate economic as well as social value while remaining sustainable within their economic, their environmental, and their social domains."

We spoke to Ioannou at his crowded office in the Regency splendor of London Business School.

When did you first get interested in this sort of area, and what was the evolution of your thinking?

You have intellectual curiosity as an academic, but then there is that moment when you find a field, a question, a domain that resonates and you say this is what I really would like to explore in more detail. In my journey I went all the way from game theory to industrial economics and then to management, a bit of technology and innovation, and then I started doing work in sustainability.

I trained as an economist and found that quite insufficient as a background for understanding business. The CSR movement sparked my interest because it is a question that essentially puts the role of business and the role of management well beyond the economic domain where it has traditionally resided. It was a time when organizations were engaging in domains beyond the economic, but as academics, we still had a huge gap in understanding where business was headed and what business was doing.

The rise of CSR is an opportunity for academia. Typically we wait for a phenomenon to play out and then come back and conduct a kind of academic CSI: we see the remains of what's happened and try to understand the phenomenon. I think academia has a much larger role to play in understanding phenomena as they evolve or as they're happening as opposed to after the event.

There's a big risk in doing things that are not exactly considered mainstream in academia and trying to publish them. In academia it's evolving, it's definitely growing in importance, because you see schools with endowed chairs in sustainability, there is a business and environment center at Harvard Business School, and so on. This reflects the evolution of sustainability as a field. This is not to say that it doesn't find any resistance, but it's certainly not as peripheral or as looked down on as it used to be 10 or 20 years ago.

There's more media coverage around CSR, and a lot of companies pay lip service to it and use it for PR

purposes—greenwashing—yet some companies are genuinely doing interesting things; it is a curious mix.
CSR comes with moral baggage. Even if some companies only pay lip service to it, and I agree that there are many that do, it's worth exploring. Why are they doing this? Are there some that are not paying lip service? If there are, why are they not paying lip service?

As academics we don't go in to find a positive or a negative relationship. We just explore the phenomenon, and then we ask whether our current management theories are enough to explain what we observe or are we missing something? Maybe the lip service, the greenwashing, and so on, may be explained, but if we move beyond that and say well, even if there are only three companies in the world that are meaningfully trying to engage, can our theories explain how they are engaging and what the impact is going to be? We do understand something about greenwashing, but I don't think we yet understand a lot about how companies truly integrate social and environmental issues and the impact of that integration for the companies themselves as well as their broader role in civil society.

Explaining what is happening as it happens in a useful way for a business audience as opposed to doing the academic CSI is a major shift for business school academics.
I would say so. It has to be done with caution on several fronts. One needs to be acutely aware of the kind

of data one uses and what kind of limitations that data has. The other thing is to maintain integrity and also manage expectations. It may be wrongly perceived as advocacy rather than simply reporting on the data analyzed. That's one of the risks, but it is worth the risk as long as you manage it cautiously and conservatively.

In which direction is your research heading?
There are one or two domains. One is the domain of innovation: understanding whether environmental or social innovation is different from traditional technology innovation and, if so, in what ways. That's a project I'm working on with George Serafeim from Harvard Business School, essentially trying to answer the question, What are the drivers of environmental innovation? Is it stakeholder engagement? Is it the longer-term time horizons that perhaps allow for more experimentation?

In talking to people about sustainability, a lot of them invoke this notion that it's a different kind of innovation, it's a different domain of problems and therefore a different domain of solutions. There is talk of inclusive innovation and so on. There isn't enough work out there exploring this particular link—between sustainability and innovation—and trying to understand if maybe there is something different.

The second domain is one where I am working with my London Business School colleague Donal Crilly. We want to understand the role of cognition, how boards or top management teams think in terms of sustainability and financial performance. In a lot of people's minds, social performance or environmental performance and financial performance are conflicting objectives. They see a trade-off between the two. To the extent that they are conflicting objectives, we ask how managers or top management teams perceive those objectives and how some of them are able to reconcile them and create companies that have high financial and social and environmental performance.

The challenge is this idea of trying to understand a company's self-image versus how it is perceived by external audiences and how this affects economic and social and environmental performance. The long-term plan is to rigorously compare a company's self-image about sustainability through its sustainability reports with the way an investment analyst perceives the role of the company in a given industry.

If a company's self-image about what it's doing in this domain is 100 percent in accordance with what analysts think, one would expect the analysts to reward it. This is just one example of where this line of work might go. The broader question is the company's self-image and its understanding of the social and environmental issues versus the external audience's expectations of, let's say, that specific industry.

When you go out and talk to executives, do they understand these issues now in a way they didn't before, do you think?

I think on average, yes. The thing that I see all the time is that there's an extreme variation. There are companies that will just ignore these issues, companies that will try to do the bare minimum. But increasingly companies understand that at the very minimum they should always be pursuing efficiency initiatives. A lot of the initiatives around sustainability (e.g., energy and water efficiency) are cost-saving. I think the mean is moving in that direction, though you can debate if the speed is fast enough.

One of the ideas you are interested in is that of the circular economy. Is it just too off-puttingly ambitious for companies?

No, I don't think so. There is no question that to the extent that businesses will contribute toward tackling the world's problems, they have to be ambitious. Isn't it ambitious when Unilever says that by 2020 it wants to make the lives of half a billion people healthier? We hear these kinds of ambitious targets almost on a daily basis. The circular economy provides a path, based on science, engineering, and design principles, and as much as it is ambitious, it also gives a solid path on how one's able to achieve this.

With the challenge of the social and environmental domain in terms of climate change, inequality, and all those big issues we're facing today, I don't think there is one solution, one business model that will automatically and magically solve all of them.

What we're witnessing is a period of experimentation in which new business models, products, and services are coming on the horizon and are being evaluated. It is not that we address these issues or come up with business models as a matter of luxury, but that it is a matter of necessity, and I think this will increasingly be the case.

What gets you out of bed in the morning, then? What's the motivation? It's January, you're in London, you're going into your office at London Business School: What's your motivation?

I like doing research; that's why I am in this profession. I enjoy the days when I know that whether I'll go to my office or it's going to be me and my laptop at a Starbucks, I'll be looking at the data and exploring interesting questions. The outcome is rewarding: you learn something new. I don't want to overphilosophize, but we are in the business of producing knowledge, and with these new pieces of knowledge, no matter how small they are, discovering them through the process of research is rewarding.

The Future Is Circular

One of the ideas likely to shape the future demonstrates the wide-ranging, eclectic, and unpredictable nature of new business ideas. The 2013 Breakthrough Idea Award at the Thinkers50, presented by Deepa Prahalad in honor of her father, C. K. Prahalad, was given to the Ellen MacArthur Foundation for its work in bringing the idea of the circular economy to the world.

The circular economy champions a virtuous circle in which, according to one of its originators, Walter Stahel, "the goods of today are used as the resources of tomorrow at yesterday's prices." It is a system in which restoring and regenerating resources is designed as part of the system rather than as a neat but optional extra. The circular economy challenges corporations to think in circular rather than linear terms about their supply chains, manufacturing processes, material flows, and business models as well as the lives of their products.

Crucially, the circular economy does not talk about *consumers* of durable goods but *users*. The argument behind the circular economy is that the linear, consumer-led economy is intrinsically a destroyer of value—whether through its use of energy or other raw materials or a lack of reusability—at all stages. The traditional value chain leaks value at every link.

The circular economy is intended to decouple economic growth from resource constraints by design. Material flows are classified in two ways: biological materials designed to reenter the biosphere safely and technical materials designed to circulate at high quality without entering the biosphere. Effectively, waste is designed out of the system and materials or components no longer required in their place of origin are "metabolized" elsewhere in the economy.

Today, the concept of the circular economy may seem ambitious, perhaps far-fetched, but history suggests that such challenging ideas have the potential to become real and have a huge practical impact. Ideas change the world. The challenge for all in business is to identify the ideas that can best help themselves and their organizations.

In Circles

At age 18 Ellen MacArthur sailed around the United Kingdom single-handedly. She went on to finish second in the 2001 Vendée Globe solo round-the-world race and broke the world record for the fastest solo circumnavigation in 2005.

In the years after her world record, MacArthur remained involved in sailing. But through her sailing experiences, visiting the remote island of South Georgia, and a thirst for knowledge, MacArthur became fascinated by the economic and resource challenges facing the global economy. She announced her retirement from racing in 2009 and in 2010 launched the Ellen MacArthur Foundation.

The foundation works to accelerate the transition to a circular economy, a different economic model based on a virtuous circle in which the goods of today are used as the resources of tomorrow.

We met Dame Ellen MacArthur at the foundation's headquarters in Cowes on the Isle of Wight.

> *Various people were involved in the genesis of the concept of the circular economy.*
> Yes, I think Walter Stahel, the economist, wrote his first book on the performance economy the year I was born. He's absolutely phenomenal. Bill McDonough and Michael Braungart, an American architect and designer and a German chemist, pioneered cradle to

cradle. Then there's people like Janine Benyus, who has been instrumental in the field of biomimicry.

The first time I came across this concept was during my journey of learning.

A journey of learning?

Very much so. Being an around-the-world sailor is fairly specific in many ways even though you have to learn many skills, from understanding the weather to first aid to sailing. Economics wasn't even a subject you could study at my school, so I had absolutely no idea about global economics. It was a long journey of learning.

For me it was kicked off by the question of resources. On a boat you have finite resources, and you realize what finite means. Translate that to the global economy and you realize there are some big challenges: 3.5 billion new middle-class consumers coming online, the population increasing, more and more demand for resources. We've seen a century of price declines erased in 10 years. Economists don't seem to think that's going to change because there's more and more demand for commodities. And for me the question was, So what works?

It was a journey similar to my goal, from the age of four, of sailing around the world. I had this goal and had no idea how to make it happen, but I knew where I wanted to get to. It was difficult, challenging, amazing, and it was an adventure, but I knew where I was going, so every decision I made took me one step closer.

With the circular economy I saw a diagram in a book by Ken Webster (now the head of innovation at the foundation). Suddenly there was this idea of a cycle. For me it made sense. It was a different way of looking at things.

Effectively, a circular economy is a model for an industrial economy in which global material flows fit within one of two cycles—stuff that biodegrades and stuff that doesn't—all running ultimately on renewable energy.

For me, this was the first seed. Suddenly, I thought this could work. This is an economy that could run in the long term. At that stage we had absolutely no idea of the economics. It made sense from a materials flow perspective and from an energy perspective, but we had no idea whether it would cost three times more than a current linear product. We had no idea.

Where did the term the circular economy *come from?*
The actual term came from Chinese law. It's in the eleventh and twelfth five-year plans that China is working toward a circular economy.

In your book Full Circle, *there was a sense you were more frightened of your journey of learning than of the actual physical danger of being in the Southern Ocean.*
There's no fear of being in the Southern Ocean. It is stressful sometimes, but it's an amazing place to be.

I'd be there like that if I could again. It's incredible. Yes, you're frightened at sea sometimes, absolutely, but you're also frightened in a car sometimes. There are certain choices that are more frightening than others, of course. But for me stepping into this space was about the fear of the unknown.

And did you have any sense where it was going? You looked at farming.

I looked at everything!

I'd learned a huge amount about sailing in a relatively short time by asking questions of anybody and everybody. It didn't matter if it was taking the engine to pieces, changing the circuit board in a computer, sewing my arm up, or administering drugs because you're 2,500 miles from the nearest town. You learn all that stuff. It's a very broad range of learning.

Actually, the winner of the race is not necessarily the fastest sailor. The winner of the race is someone who is a fast sailor but is able to keep the boat on track, maintain his or her energy level for three months, look at and understand the weather, make the decisions, and repair the boat himself or herself. It's a whole range of skills that I picked up and learned because there was this goal of racing around the world, which I was living for.

Sailing to me had been everything. It had been the one thing that had driven everything in my life and every decision took me one stage closer to that point of sailing around the world, but this was different. This wasn't about my goal to sail around the world; this was about something that was so huge that I almost couldn't comprehend it.

There must have been offers to do other things.
There were lots of offers to get involved with other people's initiatives, but nothing sat right because I needed to understand it properly before I made any decisions about what I was going to do.

That understanding came as a result of working with people at the foundation. You ask questions, go to meetings, and speak to people, and your understanding builds. What fascinated me was the systems change. It was the big picture. Obviously there's lots of small detail in the big picture, but if you can't fix the big picture, you're always fighting fires.

Where I became fascinated with the big picture was through many of the little things I came across. Take farming and fertilizer, for example. Fertilizer is becoming more and more expensive, and farmers are relying on subsidies. Most fertilizers come from minerals that are dug out of the ground and are finite. The biological material in food waste, in human waste, in agricultural waste doesn't go back to the farms. For billions of years that's gone back to the land. Now we've broken that, so the value is lost. What fascinates me is that if you look at the big picture, where are these materials, where does the value lie, how can this system function?

If you look at the system and ask, How can we redesign it so that the fertilizer can go back to the farms, suddenly you're not having a conversation with farmers and you're not having a conversation around mining specifically; you're looking at a systems change.

The more work we did with McKinsey, the more it showed that there's a huge economic benefit in shifting toward that model. You take one metric ton of food waste and it's got $6 of fertilizer in it, $18 of heat, and $26 of electricity. Currently most of that's lost. It is composted and covers landfills. There's so much value there. You're creating gas, which helps with energy. You're creating fertilizer that helps farmers. You're creating heat, which helps from a general individual housing perspective. All from something that at the moment leaks out of the system. That systems element fascinated me.

What does success look like?
A functioning circular economy.

But that's a big change for you. It's the difference between going from A to B in a yacht and sailing around the world, where the goals are crystal clear.
Yes, but it's just a different racecourse. You still know exactly what you're trying to get to. You still know that you're trying to shift the economy from being a linear one to a circular one. What we've tried to do is pull the biggest levers that we can as a small organization, such as working with McKinsey, the World Economic Forum, and the best universities in the world. The

Schmidt-MacArthur Fellowship program means working with the students but also with academics.

If you ask me what the goal is, it's to shift the overall economy from a linear to a circular one. How fast that can happen, I don't have the answer. There are a lot of companies that won't survive as the linear economy continues. The speed of the change will be relative to the realization by companies that there's a better way of doing things and the benefits that brings. That's why we put the economic reports together to say there is an economic opportunity of in excess of a trillion U.S. dollars in this space to do this now.

This is happening at speed all over the world; whether it's flagged as the circular economy or not is another question. What we've tried to do is give it a rationale and a framework, pull these ideas together, put numbers to it, and say this opportunity is there for the taking right now.

Do you think of yourself as a leader?

I think of myself as a team player, but I'm happy to put my neck on the line if that's needed. I'm not someone who has to be at the front; I'd actually rather be at the back. But if the best way to make it happen is to stand on a stage and talk about something, I'll be there without a breath of hesitation. But it's about everyone in the team playing the best roles that he or she can. And I think we have a phenomenal group here of people from different backgrounds, countries, and experiences who all put their absolute utmost into what they're doing.

When I look back to the sailing and the around-the-world record, the fondest memory for me without a shadow of a doubt is teamwork. I worked with an amazing team of people. You may spend 71 days, 14 hours, 18 minutes, and 33 seconds on your own, but actually for years you work with a team to design the boat, build the boat, put the boat together, trial the boat, test the boat, sail halfway around the world on the boat, and prepare for records. Those guys and girls you work with in many cases have your life in their hands. Working with them and having that amazing team spirit for me was what the project was all about. It wasn't about being on my own; it wasn't about me. I crossed the finish line on my own and felt absolutely nothing about having broken the record until they got on board, and then that was really quite powerful.

One and Only

In the 1990s Tom Peters was the first to champion the idea of brand you. In an increasingly competitive employment marketplace, Peters argued, people needed to develop and communicate their own brands.

At the time (August 1997) Peters's article "The Brand Called You" made the cover of *Fast Company*. The entire idea of brand you seemed to appeal to a self-confident elite of West Coast whiz kids. Now the idea is mainstream. It is expected that people will market themselves in one way or another to be promoted or get a job in the first place.

But how? If you are the brand, what are the implications? Among those most helpfully making sense of the practicalities of personal branding is Dorie Clark, an adjunct professor of business administration at Duke University's Fuqua School of Business. Clark is a former presidential campaign spokeswoman and author of *Reinventing You: Define Your Brand, Imagine Your Future* (2013).

One of the most intriguing aspects of your career was your time working with Howard Dean's presidential campaign in 2004.

It was a great ride. When I started with the campaign, it was quite small. We were all in a tiny office in Vermont. There were about 20 staff members nationally, and by the end of it Howard Dean had gone from an obscure footnote of a candidate to being the front-runner to once again ending up as an also-ran and having to drop out. It was a tremendous whirlwind and a very big learning opportunity.

What did you learn from the experience?

The basic thing that I learned, which I think remains quite valuable, is that 2004 was really a tipping point in terms of the world of media and communications. We were literally the first presidential campaign that had a blog. So number one was the ever-increasing pace of the media cycle. Number two was how to deal with a media and communications landscape where reporters are not the only players. You have bloggers, and you have citizen journalists; there's a whole raft of ways to get your message across, and in fact our campaign became a content producer. That was a new way of thinking about things. As the media landscape gets more and more crowded, you have to find new ways to get your message out.

In politics you have to do that while people are constantly trying to throw you off message, trying to attack you, to get others to misinterpret what you're doing. It gave me a really good sense of what can go wrong, how to mitigate problems, and how to play good defense and offense in terms of messaging and communications.

The other interesting thing about your background is your spell at Harvard Divinity School. Does that still influence your thinking?

Yes. I loved my time there. I went straight after being an undergraduate and was still very much enmeshed in a lot of philosophical questions. I'm really interested in how people make meaning of their world and their lives, so that was something that I wanted to study and wanted to learn more about.

The other motivating factor, which actually ties in more with the political work that I did, was that at the time there was a lot of energy in the United States around the religious right getting active in politics, and as someone who cared about politics and about the direction of the country, I wanted to understand that phenomenon, to understand where they were coming from.

After that you were involved in making films and worked as a journalist.

I consider myself as sort of an accident of history, at the vanguard of discovering some of the truths of the modern economy! Not necessarily because I wanted to or because I was so smart but because I was 22 years old at the right time and I kept losing my job and had to find out why. That quest, fortunately I think, has led me to understand some things about how people can construct a future for themselves that hopefully is more satisfying and enables them to make a bigger contribution. That's what I try to share.

In many ways what you're doing now is to some extent journalistic. You're asking questions, distilling lots of information, and turning it into something that resonates with as big an audience as possible.

Absolutely. It's journalism not tethered to a particular institution or organization, but yes, it comes from a very journalistic place.

What do you describe yourself as? On your website it says "Marketing Strategy Consultant," but that doesn't quite seem right.

Yes, for me that's kind of a blanket term that I can insert a whole lot of other meanings into. There are four principal ways that I spend my time and make money. Consulting is one, speaking, teaching for business schools, and then writing. I feel like "Marketing

Strategy Consultant" is sort of broad enough and non-descript enough that it encompasses all of those things.

An increasing number of the people we talk to are thought leaders and agenda setters who are independent.
Yes. I'm an autonomy junkie! I do love having relationships with lots of people and entities, but it's nice to be able to set your own agenda running your own business.

How do you explain your personal brand?
When I'm talking about my personal brand, I think of myself as someone who is hopefully insightful, fun and funny, and really committed to trying to find ways to increase access to opportunity. What's really exciting for me about personal branding and the whole ethos of it is the fact that it really is an egalitarian force in the world—when it's done right.

Obviously, you have all kinds of people who make fun of the concept of personal branding. They think that it's egotism run rampant or some kind of manipulation or fakery. I actually think it's far from that. It is a way in which people can really express their value. It's a way in which people can really express who they are and make sure that people understand that and grasp what kind of contribution they can make.

In a world where you can do that, where people are really appreciated for who they are, that's tremendously powerful. It's no longer about credentials or connections. It's about merit. That's what I think is pretty cool.

"An egalitarian force" is a great phrase, isn't it? Because it always seems that personal branding is the preserve of the few rather than the opportunity for the many.

Yes. In some ways it has been like that. That's why I like to evangelize for it. Everyone has a personal brand: his or her reputation. It's just a question of whether you want to think about it and acknowledge it and actively try to take control of it or if you want to just leave it to the fates. But if you are willing to take control of it, it can do really powerful things for your career and your life.

Isn't there a danger that you'll become overly worried about what other people think?

There's always that danger. You want to be mindful of it, but I don't think that it inherently puts you in that position. Actually, on the contrary, it's really about elucidating who you are; understanding that and communicating it effectively.

Personal branding is not an outside-in phenomenon in which you say: What does the world want? How can I be more like that? How can I look like that or pretend to be like that? Instead it's an inside-out phenomenon in which you really dig down and figure out who you are, what you care about, what you want to do, what you can contribute to the world. And then you get the rest of the world to see that.

Historically, the reverse has happened in organizations. You fitted your personal brand to the organization.
Yes. I mean, that's the story of the twentieth century. I think the story of the twenty-first century is overturning that completely, because we know that organizations don't need any more yes men. In fact, organizations themselves are picking up on that fact. They need creative, entrepreneurial thinkers who are willing to say: Wait a minute, let's do something differently. Let's try it differently. We need a new perspective.

What's the thing people most commonly get wrong or simply don't understand about personal branding?
The most common thing that people get wrong is that they make the assumption that other people are following their career more closely than they are, and so consequently they don't take the time to create a real, coherent, crisp narrative that explains who they are, where they've been, and how that adds value to where they're going.

People assume that other people will just intuit that or grasp it, and most people aren't paying that close attention to you. You need to be very deliberate in thinking about it and articulating it to others; otherwise they will simply guess, and they will probably guess wrong. That means you will miss out on opportunities.

*So it's about having a clear idea of what your story is
and then articulating it?*

Yes. And thinking of my own story, there's a reason
that this is interesting to me. I was a philosophy major
as an undergraduate. My graduate degree is in the-
ology, which on the surface might be a weird background for someone who is writing business books
and is a marketing strategist. In my mind it makes a
lot of sense, and I try to articulate that to others. You
hear it so much that it's almost a cliché, but they say:
"Personal branding's about authenticity." Well, I think
that's really true in a literal sense. For me, the same
thing that drove me to study philosophy and religion
drives me to study personal branding.

It's about who people are fundamentally. What
is their role in the world? What can they contribute?
What are we here for? And if you know that, that is
an almost unstoppable force. But you're right. Most
people don't know that. They don't go that deep. They
don't think about it. That means that their opportunities are limited and their satisfaction with their professional life is often limited.

*Isn't it true that only a few people actually have a
clear idea of what their role in the universe is? It's a
lot easier said than done, isn't it?*

Absolutely, and that's why one of the things that I talk
about is that in the process of trying to discover your
narrative and figure out where you want to be and what
you want to be doing, there is a role for war stories.

We know far too much about ourselves. It's really hard to drill down to that level of clarity, because we have way too many inputs. We cannot see the trees because we have this massive forest in front of us. What I suggest to people is to start at the granular level and work their way up. You can't do it top down. It's too confusing.

Start by thinking about or writing down some of the war stories that matter most to you: the times in your life when you really felt something click or you learned something, the moment in your professional life when you said: "This is really interesting." It's a story that you think about enough to repeat to others.

If you set enough of those stories down on paper, you can actually begin to extrapolate what you care about and what you want your brand to be. It's really hard to do it in the reverse, but if you work your way up from the stories, it can help you see what resonates.

It must be a function of age as well. A 55-year-old white Anglo-Saxon senior executive must find this a difficult message, although perhaps the ones who have succeeded are the ones who actually have done the personal branding.

Age is a really interesting question. I wrote a piece for the *Harvard Business Review* called "How to Reinvent Yourself After 50," and that got a lot of pickup. A common objection that I hear from people is "Oh, this is nice if you're 20. It's nice if you're 40. It's not so helpful if you're 55. What can I do? I'm stuck. I've got my brand; I don't have time to go back to school. Am I doomed, as it were?"

There are things that people can absolutely do at every age. Most of the things that I suggest in *Reinventing You* are things that people can do regardless of age, regardless of income. I'm trying to suggest things like this: Well, if you are missing some skills, think about taking a class. Don't commit yourself to something that takes years and hundreds of thousands of dollars. Try the minimum viable solution and then try other things. Try volunteering. Try blogging. Try job shadowing. These are all things that anyone can do as long as he or she is willing to try it.

Where does the work go next?

The next thing that I'm working on is about thought leadership and how to become a recognized expert in one's field. For me, I view it as a continuation of the work I did in *Reinventing You*. That book is for people who have big goals, who want something more in their careers. Maybe they want to change jobs. Maybe they want to move up in their company but feel they are stymied because people do not perceive the full value they can contribute. They need to somehow reshape that to get to the place they want to go.

This next piece of work is for people who are already in the place where they want to be. They know where they want to make their mark. But the question is: How do you get the maximum impact from your ideas? How do you really get recognized for what you want to say? More and more this is becoming a really fragmented marketplace.

Even if you have good ideas and bold thinking, it's hard to get attention for it. So how do you do it? I have interviewed a lot of cool thought leaders, many of whom are in the Thinkers50 orbit—Seth Godin, Tom Peters, Rita McGrath, Dan Pink, and people like that—and I have tried in many ways to reverse engineer what has made them successful, to begin to think about how regular people could apply those principles in their lives. My goal is essentially to reach the kind of people who are really excited about making their mark in the world, entrepreneurs or executives who really want to make a difference and want to be known for their ideas.

Give and Take

Bringing a fascinating new perspective to personal branding and the contribution of individuals is Adam Grant. Grant is the youngest full professor at the Wharton School and has been recognized as Wharton's highest-rated teacher and one of Malcolm Gladwell's favorite social science writers. Before taking up a career in academia, Grant was the advertising director at Let's Go Publications, an all-American springboard diver, and a professional magician.

In his bestselling book *Give and Take*, he examines how being generous with our time and expertise affects our personal success. Grant identifies three groups of people: givers, takers, and matchers. Givers are inclined to give favors generously, whereas matchers look for a quid pro quo. Takers, in contrast, are in it for themselves and help others only if there is something more in it for themselves. Interestingly, Grant's research indicates that the most successful people are often givers, though givers run the risk of being doormats for others.

Grant's studies have been highlighted in a number of other bestselling books, including *Quiet* by Susan Cain, *Drive* and *To Sell Is Human* by Dan Pink, and *David and Goliath* by Malcolm Gladwell.

> *How did you get interested in the subject of give and take?*
>
> I've always been interested in what makes some people more successful than others, and when I started doing research on that, there were three categories that came up consistently: hard work, talent, and luck. I was struck by the fact that those were all individual factors but we were all working in a connected world. As I dug more into that question, it was really interesting to see that there were so many people who said I really care about giving back, but I'm going to amass as much success and influence and wealth as I can first and then I'll start trying to help others.
>
> I thought that was backward.
>
> *Didn't you find that people who give back are more successful? So good guys can finish first, which is a life-affirming discovery.*
>
> Yes it is, although I always want to convey that enthusiasm with a bit of caution, because there are about as many givers who sink to the bottom. But yes, it's

pretty exciting that people who put others first most of the time can actually end up finishing first themselves.

How did you go about researching it?
The research comes in lots of different flavors. Some of the most compelling and rigorous studies are the ones that actually ask people to rate one another and gather 360-degree feedback anonymously on whether they tend to give more than they get, trade fairly evenly, or receive more favors than they contribute to others. When you do that, you can track over time what happens to various objectives, viewing performance metrics as a function of the balance between giving and taking. You can look at everything from engineering productivity, to sales revenue, to grades in medical school.

What sorts of small favors are we talking about? Somebody making an introduction and not necessarily expecting anything in return?
Introductions can be acts of giving.

Other big categories would be knowledge sharing, mentoring, helping, providing feedback, and teaching skills. Sometimes it's as simple as showing up early or staying a bit late to support your colleagues.

When you looked at people's profiles, you found that there were three distinct types: the givers, the takers, and the matchers. Can you say a little about each of those types?

These styles of interaction turn out to be universal as far as we can tell across industries and cultures. The people who operate primarily as takers are always trying to get as much as possible from others. They never want to give anything back unless they have to.

A fairly typical taker would be somebody who ends up claiming all the interesting, visible, important projects, leaving the grunt work for everyone else, and still manages to walk away with the lion's share of the credit.

At the other end of the spectrum, we have the people I call givers, and I've been really working to redefine giving as not just about philanthropy or volunteering but, as you said, about these everyday acts of helping others with no strings attached.

The givers are the people who will volunteer to provide help, make introductions, share knowledge, and be mentors without asking for anything in return from the people they help.

Then, in the middle, we have most of us: matchers. In the majority of our interactions, most people operate like matchers, trying to keep an even balance of giving and taking, quid pro quo. If I were a matcher and I did you a favor, I would expect an equal one back, and if you did me a favor, I might feel I was in debt until I had settled the score.

If most of us are in the middle, there are more of the matchers than the others. How does it break down among the three groups?

It varies from one organization, industry, and culture to another. But across the board, the data that have been gathered suggest that on average about 55 to 60 percent of the population are matchers and the remainder are a pretty even mix of givers and takers.

If we're givers in one part of our lives, are we predisposed to be givers in all areas? Or might we be givers at work and takers in another scenario?

People do fluctuate quite a bit. The most common pattern is to be a giver at home and a matcher at work.

If you asked people who were parents, for example, to think of the last time their kid asked for a ride to school or football practice, not many parents would say, "What have you done for me lately?" to their children. With families and friends, people like to help and rarely keep score.

But in the workplace, a lot of people worry that other people are takers, and so they say it's a dog-eat-dog competitive place: if I don't put myself first, nobody else will.

Are there rules of thumb for spotting the three types? Are there dead giveaways in these situations, or is it just a case of figuring out after a few interactions where somebody is?

Most people think that they're very good at recognizing who is a giver and who is a taker. Unfortunately, the evidence shows that until you know someone well, most people do no better than random chance. One of the biggest reasons we get fooled is a personality trait called agreeableness.

Agreeable people tend to be warm and friendly and nice and welcoming and polite, whereas more disagreeable people are likely to be critical, skeptical, and challenging with others. Most of us associate these personality traits with giving and taking. If you're a nice guy—if you're agreeable—I will assume that you're a giver, and if you're a little bit more tough and gruff in your interaction, I may assume that you're a taker.

Yet when you look at the data, the correlation between agreeable-disagreeable and giving-taking is basically zero. Agreeableness and disagreeableness is about your outer veneer, whereas giving and taking is about your inner motives, your intentions.

Is agreeableness what we sometimes call charm?

Exactly. Of course, there are agreeable givers and disagreeable takers, but we forget that there are disagreeable givers, who are the most undervalued people in an organization. These are the people who are not always pleasant to interact with; they often are described as prickly or overly harsh in their judgments. But they have other people's best interests at heart. They're often the ones who are willing to blow the whistle, ask the tough questions, and play devil's advocate in the service of organizational goals even though they may be not that easy to deal with on an everyday basis.

The people we have to watch out for are the agreeable takers, whom I call the fakers. They're nice to your face but perfectly willing to stab you in the back.

As individuals, do we select a strategy? Do we decide ourselves, I'm going to be a taker or I'm going to be a giver, or are we predisposed to one or the other?

It turns out to be a little bit of both. There is such a thing as being good-natured. There are some people who are born or raised to feel a strong sense of empathy or duty or social responsibility and others who obviously have a different DNA or upbringing. But the nice thing is that these are choices we make in every interaction we have with another person. Even if your default is to be a taker, you could walk into your next interaction and decide, You know what—this time I'm going to propose an even trade or even offer something without asking for something back.

There are plenty of people who make deliberate and intentional choices to shift the level of trust they have depending on who they are dealing with and how independent they are. It is something that goes beyond your personality.

That's good news: there's hope for all of us. If we are going to adopt a strategy, how do we ensure that we're the ones who rise to the top rather than ending up being a doormat?

That's a great question. I think it comes down to being thoughtful in three ways: about who, how, and when you give. The givers who get themselves in trouble are the ones who are constantly helping takers. You can waste a lot of your time and energy helping people who are very selfish. It is easy to get burned and burned out, so the idea is to focus on having givers and matchers around you. The beauty of helping matchers is that they tend to feel really motivated to pay it back and make sure that what goes around comes around.

The givers actually do less of that, but they really focus on paying it forward, allowing whatever you contribute to spread.

As far as the how is concerned, the basic advice is to be a specialist, not a generalist when you give. The givers who try to be all things to all people end up spreading themselves really thin, and it's not very efficient or energizing to help in hundreds of different ways. Successful givers focus on one or two ways of helping that they're uniquely good at and that they enjoy. Specialized giving is less distracting and exhausting, and they can develop a reputation as people who have a distinctive skill set that they're willing and able to share.

The third part is the when. Failed givers are the people who are willing to drop anything at any time to fulfill a request, whereas successful givers block out time in their calendars to get their own goals accomplished, finish their own work. They have separate windows set aside to be helpful.

So this is a managed process. It is strategic giving. It isn't just default, all-the-time, unthinking giving. Nice as that may be, it's probably not that effective in the long run.

Yes, that's right. I think if you become too strategic about it, you slip into becoming a taker or a matcher. But yes, I think this is about being thoughtful, about saying a giver wants to have a high return on investment. That really means giving where you can have the biggest impact.

This doesn't sound like good news for takers, because if we're matchers or we're givers, the people we want to avoid are the takers, presumably.

Yes, that's right; the matchers are especially motivated to punish takers because they violate a sense of justice and fairness. Smart givers learn over time to be more cautious in dealing with takers, so I do think it's bad news for takers. Of course, there are some people who are so talented or so hardworking that they get away with being takers, but most of us don't have that luxury. The data suggest anyway that as the world shifts to become one that's more about collaboration and service than it has been in the past, it's going to be harder and harder for takers to succeed.

What would be your advice to someone coming into the world of work about career networking and how to get on?

The first thing to do is become a little bit more attuned to other people's styles. As you encounter givers and matchers, obviously you try to surround yourself with more of those people, because you can trust them to have your best interests at heart. You can also give a little bit more freely without worrying about the consequences.

One way to test the water is to do what the serial entrepreneur Adam Rifkin calls the five-minute favor. If you're motivated to give, to be helpful and make a difference, which most people are, you don't have to be Mother Teresa or Gandhi. In fact, that's not sustainable for most of us. Instead of worrying about getting sucked into extremely time-consuming acts of helping and giving, you should look for ways to add high value to others at a low personal cost. If you can add a few more five-minute favors each week, it's a great way to contribute more value to other people without making a personal sacrifice.

Do you practice this personally?

I strive to as much as possible. You can't study these kinds of dynamics without trying to practice a little bit of what you preach.

Do you have a plan that you follow?

I try to do a lot of chunking, and so there are days when I don't help very many people outside my family because I'm focused on teaching, writing, research, or other activities to which I've committed. There are other days when I'll set aside time and help as many students as I can and see what I can do to support my colleagues as well. I find that dividing it that way is extremely helpful.

Through writing *Give and Take*, I learned to be a lot clearer about my own priorities: family first, students second, colleagues third, everybody else fourth. When somebody reaches out, I know that I'm going to respond faster when it's a student than when it's a colleague. That's why I became a professor—to help and inspire students, not to make a difference for fellow professors.

When somebody reaches out who doesn't fall into one of those first few categories, I ask myself: Is this really the best use of my time, or can I refer you to a book or another person or a resource that can answer your question better than I can?

There's no doubt that there are some very selfish people who do get on in life. What sets the alarm bells ringing for you?

There are a couple of sneaky ways that takers manage to fool other people. One is a pattern that I call kissing up, kicking down. Takers are really good fakers when dealing with powerful people, because it's advantageous for influential people to think that you're generous. But it's a lot of work to fake concern for others in all your interactions, and so takers tend to let their guard down a little bit with peers and subordinates. If you really want to know somebody's style, don't ask his or her boss; ask the people who work across from and below that person.

Also, takers often give first and then make a bigger ask later. A lot of us have learned to have an alarm go off when we've just met somebody and all of a sudden that person is overeager to help us. Sometimes, because they're charming or because they manage to ingratiate, we get fooled by them. That's something we have to be careful about.

Third, over time, takers give off more of a transactional impression. Initially takers are quite charming because they know that's what they need to do to get ahead. But you will find that you hear from them only when they want something.

Are there lessons from this for organizations? Are there things that organizations can do culturally or that the CEO can do to try to ensure that a greater percentage of the population plays the giving game rather than the taking game or the matching game?

Any one style used inflexibly is risky. You do have to get smart at adjusting and adapting without losing sight of your values and your character. The evidence suggests that the best thing to do when you encounter a taker is to operate more like a matcher, and it becomes very much tit for tat: if this person gives, I will give back, but I'm not going to do it without some kind of quid pro quo. But a lot of givers feel really uncomfortable with that and don't want to have to be constantly keeping score. One way to navigate this dilemma is instead of asking the taker to help you, ask him or her to help somebody else. In that way, you're holding the taker accountable but don't feel like you're stepping out of your own value system.

The nice thing is that if you're a giver, an ask feels like helping when it's on behalf of someone else.

What's next for you? What are you working on?

I'm not going to be one of those people who write 19 sequels on the same topic. I love asking a big question that's interesting and has practical significance and then really trying to tackle it, and so my next book will probably approach a different topic. But something I am working on right now is one of the unanswered questions from the book: What does it take to turn a taker into a giver?

Can the tiger change its stripes, and what are the conditions that produce those kinds of shifts?

Any early signals or clues so far?

There are a couple of initial patterns that are coming out. The data suggest that it's very hard to convince people that they should change their values, but they're a lot more likely to convince themselves. Takers do seem to change a little bit in the giver direction when they are actually advocating for the importance of giving. Rather than asking a taker to think more like a giver, what I would do is get that person to try to persuade other people to act like a giver.

You spent time working as a magician? Are there parallels with what takers do?

It was one of my early exposures to psychology. The sleight of hand that magicians do is what takers pull off without anyone ever knowing that it was just a trick.

How did you get interested in magic, and do you still practice it?

I was babysitting for some kids down the street. They were very hyper, and one day they started doing magic tricks. Somebody had gotten them a magic set, and I noticed that they actually sat still and listened. I went home and learned a few tricks to keep them entertained, and I found that it was a great way, as an introvert, to come out of my shell. Then it snowballed. I don't do a lot of shows anymore, but at teaching or speaking events I often get roped into doing a couple of tricks, and I still enjoy it.

It's a useful party trick to have. Do you still classify yourself as an introvert, or would you see yourself now as an extrovert?

At heart, I'm still an introvert. I definitely prefer a good book to a party most of the time, but I also give hundreds of speeches a year.

How does that fit with being a teacher and giving speeches as a thought leader?

For much of my job, when I'm not writing and doing research, I am on stage, acting more like an extrovert.

When I poll my students, most of them guess that I'm an extrovert. I've been inspired by Susan Cain's book *Quiet* and also by the research of Brian Little. As an introvert, when I'm on stage, I'm acting out of character. I play the part of an extrovert, and it can be exhausting, but in a way I'm also doing it because of my character, because I really believe in my message and care about sharing these ideas.

It's out of my normal personality zone, but it's very much congruent with my values.

So it's authentic?
Yes. Malcolm Gladwell put it well when he said, "Speaking is not an act of extroversion—it's a performance, and many performers are hugely introverted."

CHAPTER 9

All Together Now

One big issue we haven't directly touched on in this book so far is the digitization of everything and the rise of social media. We haven't left it to last because it is an afterthought but for precisely the opposite reason. Technology affects all the issues we and the thinkers have explored up to this point in this book. It is the social and intellectual glue of our times. It has an impact on everything from organizations to leadership, from innovation to careers.

The final thinker we feature communicates this message with compelling power. Nilofer Merchant teaches innovation at Stanford and Santa Clara universities. In a meteoric 20-year career, Merchant has gone from being an administrator to becoming a

CEO and then a board member of a Nasdaq-traded company. Along the way she has gathered monikers such as "the Jane Bond of Innovation" for her ability to guide Fortune 500 and start-up companies. She is the author of two bestselling books: *The New How* (2010) and *11 Rules for Creating Value in the #SocialEra* (2012). She won the 2013 Thinkers50 Future Thinker Award.

What were some of your formative business experiences?

One of the experiences I had really early in my career was working with Steve Jobs. I did a presentation to him, and he told me that that what I was doing was going to be eliminated. It wasn't necessary, it wasn't even part of the picture, he said, and I was looking at him and thinking, "You are out of your mind," because at that time it was delivering something like 20 percent of the total revenues of Apple and 47 percent of the profit of the company.

Was he right?

He was: dead right. That's given me so much perspective because it's so easy to keep thinking that the base of revenue is what you need to protect. If anything, I now have the opposite instinct, which is that as soon as you know you're succeeding, you have to figure out how to begin building the next thing.

You can't tell how quickly the future is going to happen. But what you can know is that you need to go in that direction because all the things that you try and fail with in the meantime teach you how to get it right when the time is right. I always talk about building the innovation muscles so that you can be ready for that moment when you need to sprint.

Rita McGrath from Columbia Business School talks about the end of sustainable competitive advantage and the importance of being able to close things down as well as start things up. Do you agree?

I think she's on to something. I reviewed her manuscript probably two years ago, and she hadn't named it as *The End of Competitive Advantage* at that point. I wrote Rita a note to say that the first thing you actually have to say is to clarify what you're saying, which is that it's the end of competitive advantage, and complete that thought for business leaders, because that's what's going to help it land with people. The old operating rules are no longer the right operating rules. But yeah, I think she is right. You need to be able to wind things down or know how to transition, maybe. But mostly you need to know how to invest in the future.

Companies don't usually shut down profitable operations in order to migrate. Is that something new?

I've been doing all this work in boardrooms now for 15 years or so, and one of the things I started noticing was that all of them ask the exact same question: How much do I budget for the future development of the business? If I'm wanting to go faster in the new space, am I allocating 5 percent, am I allocating 10 or 15 percent? Give me a high, medium, low budget range so I can start thinking, at least with dollars and allocation of resources, start thinking about what's next.

Is there a correct answer to that question?
I used to show leaders indexes of companies across industries and what they were doing because quite often we had a back-channel view of what equivalent companies were doing. I would share that these guys are investing about 7, these guys are investing about 15, and five years ago what they were investing was this.

We could show them a spectrum, and that helped them act, invest in the right direction. It usually turned out that the right number was around 10 or 15 percent. If you invested more, you actually didn't get any more because the organization couldn't handle it. Inventing the future is always as much about change management as anything else, and so even if you threw more money at it, you couldn't make it go any faster.

You are increasingly well known as a business thinker, but you are also a practitioner. Your bio says you have personally launched more than 100 products, which netted $18 billion. Can you tell us about that part of your career and some of the products you were involved in?
Sure. Let's go back to the Apple story. I was involved in pricing Apple products in different parts of the marketing mix at a relatively early point in my career. Then at one point I was asked to solve a problem that the business division had. The GM [general manager]

of the Americas at that time just handed me a spread-sheet, and apparently, in retrospect, he'd been trying to hand it to virtually everybody. But he just tagged me, and I didn't know enough to run.

He said, There's one part of the business that is about 50 percent margin right now and making only a few million dollars. But if we could get this part to grow, it could actually sustain us with everything else, including the decline of every other part of the business. He said, Do you think you can help me solve this problem? And with the audacity of a 24- or 25-year-old, not knowing any better, I said, Sure, I can help you with that problem.

I went in to my boss and said I have no idea what I just picked up, and he said no, you don't. And I said, well, I'll figure it out. And that product line turned out to be the first $180 million of that $18 billion. This was in the early days of the web, basically preweb, and it was a matter of figuring out how to market the Apple server product, getting people to think about how to buy it.

All I did was figure out why was it currently selling well, and then try to discover whether there was a secret to that that we could use to duplicate that success. That turned out to be hugely successful and got written up in the newspapers.

What happened next?

From Apple I went to a little company called GoLive, and GoLive was the first web offering software that did HTML. We got that company successfully sold to Adobe, and I think that was a total of $4 million, and you can see how they show up in small increments.

Then I ran the North America division of Autodesk and grew that, and that was in the $300 million range.

From that point forward I worked in consulting, going into teams that were struggling with shipping a product because the price was wrong, or the value proposition was wrong, or they didn't know who the customer was, or some part of the total business proposition was so broken that they were missing their target. And so I've had a chance to do that, including Adobe's creative suite products: actually designing what that would look like as a configuration and defining a value proposition.

The funny thing is that Adobe fought that one to its end, saying nobody will buy all the stuff all together. And I told them, actually you have a bunch of incredibly loyal customers who will. And you could make it easier for them to choose you.

I've really liked working with teams, not just at the very, very top executive level but teams actually building a product and figuring out who that customer is and figuring out how to ship it. So at some point I realized I was good at figuring out what was broken pretty fast, locking in to what was missing, listening to the answers to three questions, six questions. My team used to privately say it was like watching *Name That Tune* because I could figure out the problem in five questions, four questions, three questions. Then it was just about designing a solution so that the business model was complete enough, thorough and innovative enough that it would allow the product to go out in the market successfully.

Let's talk about your book 11 Rules for Creating Value in the #SocialEra. *What are the big ideas in that book?*
The genesis of the book is telling. I'd gone to a board meeting at which I was sitting in as a guest for a Fortune 100 company to see if I wanted to join that board. I heard the chairman of the board talking about how they needed to protect their existing market, how they needed to build a bigger moat around it, how they needed to manage the efficiency of the value chain.

I was sitting there cringing. Everything they were saying seemed so viscerally wrong to me because I don't think that *any* customer is at the end of some value chain anymore. That construct is a very linear one and diminishes where value can actually come from. I came back to my desk wanting to write this e-mail, a personal thank-you for the opportunity to join the board but explaining I wouldn't be joining because I didn't think it was a good match.

But the other emotion was that I really wanted to help them. With my background in consulting being what it is, I thought, Let me see if I can actually help you see something that you can't see. I wanted to simply send them something someone else had written. I came back and looked around, and I looked at who else could have written this, and where is the argument, and I honestly couldn't find it. And it was like, gosh, it seems so obvious.

So then I reached out to some other business thinkers—friends who I thought would be the right people who would have seen it or written it and who said that customers are as much a part of the co-creation process, not just a recipient, and that the value chain construct is one of the past. Connected individuals can now connect to one another without the need for a large corporation to orchestrate their activities. Networks allow you to do what once only large centralized organizations could. If that's the case, what is the point of all these existing organizations? Networks change the nature of competition by changing who you are competing with.

And they were all shaking their heads. No one's written that, they said, but *you* should. I shook it off for two months, and then one day in this diatribe moment I wrote a 4,000-word initial take on what this argument was and sent it to my editor over at *Harvard Business Review*, and she said, "Oh, my gosh, we have to get this in the magazine right away."

I said, whoa, this is the first time I've even had the thought this clearly. How about we blog it? And that was what we did.

What was the idea behind it?

There are a few nuggets. The first point is that social is more than just media. It is an opportunity that cuts across every part of the business model. You can use it to build a product, ship a product, design a product. Every possible thing that you do in a business can be social. I've seen it in different parts. No one's actually integrated them across eight functional areas of a business, but I've seen it work. That's one big step forward.

Then the idea that's controversial, that got me known, was the argument about why Michael Porter's theories are no longer working. That was the headline of the piece. What I argue is that since connected individuals can now do what only large organizations could do before, it challenges two parts of fundamental management theory. One is the thesis of the firm— Ronald Coase's original thesis of the firm and why it actually exists. And the other one is the notion of competitive advantage.

As information and knowledge flows are pervasive, it becomes impossible to protect business by hoarding information. The challenge going forward is to figure out how to actually expose that information and allow other people to build something with you. Advantages then happen because people want to work with you and solve problems faster through their ability to scan the environment and change it.

The social era book's thesis was this idea of connected individuals being able to do what only centralized organizations could do before. The implication of that is that it changes what you do, how you do it, and then what form it takes, which changes the basis of how you compete.

Is this the death knell of large organizations? Are big corporations like GE obsolete in this new world?

I know a lot of people would like to say they are. I don't think so.

People say old companies can't innovate and small companies are more inventive. That argument is both old and wrong. Joseph Schumpeter, the noted economist, said in I believe it was 1909 that small companies were more inventive than large ones. But then in 1942, Schumpeter reversed himself and argued that big companies had more ability and incentive to invest in new products. A look at any performance measure shows that innovation can come from either size and that both arguments are oversimplifications.

The key for every firm—regardless of size—is to figure out how to consistently create value in a demanding, ever-changing market. That is hard no matter what size you are, no matter what industry you're in.

What I will say is that traditional organizations will have a very different basis. Let me give you an example. Years ago, IBM started doing something that I found truly profound, especially when I compared it with companies such as HP that didn't do it. IBM started saying our expertise isn't just what we ship, it isn't just what we build, it isn't just what we create all by ourselves. We could actually allow other people to shape that.

IBM's Smarter Planet initiative started off as an effort to say, "We should do something in the green space, but we don't know what." They asked the questions to participants really broadly, drawing on talent that was outside the firm. They were eliminating the perimeter of the firm, not trying to help with an existing problem that was defined but saying, What problems should we solve?

They changed their perspective: the parameter of the question was open, and who could participate in solving that problem was also open. And with that Smarter Planet is now making a pretty sizable contribution to the business. Now, is that enough to sustain an entire business? No, but I think it's indicative of how social can work to fuel new innovations.

Which is to say that within five years you can achieve a lot. Let's take another example. You can't do it today, but if in 5 years or 10 years I can take a picture of a jet engine and use a 3D printer type of thing to manufacture it, I no longer need to be inside your plant to know what that engine is. If I can take a picture of some functional thing and then get it to an engineer and have it produced, what is GE's role in "making" that thing? It isn't just about their ability to manufacture. It is about their ability to design it, and their know-how, and their ability to ask the right questions to customers.

I think the key shift isn't *what* you make but *how* you make it and *who* you ask the *right* questions to inform what you're thinking. IBM is one of the best at understanding how to solve really complex problems, so of course you would continue going to them, because they've done it before. That's their advantage. But it's not about defending turf or even saying we're going to keep you out. It's much more about IBM or GE saying come and build something with me.

What you're describing is co-creation as a competitive advantage. It's the opposite of building barriers to entry; it's the ability to invite people in.
Yes, instead of all the stuff going on inside your building, in your architecture, with a big moat around it, and saying please don't come here because this is ours, this is our hill that we've created and we're the castle on top of the hill, it's much more like an open playground where we invite a whole bunch of people to play and then see what we can create together. And what do we do after we have created something together? What do we do with all that stuff?

How do we sell it? How do we make money? All those other questions can come. Then you draw on talent that you couldn't get any other way. That's the advantage.

We're talking about a new model where we see organizations as social systems. You're talking about them competing with one another on the basis of how social they are.
I'm talking about moving from a closed system— closed meaning thinking about things as us versus them—to an open system that says we allow you to

play in terms of what we create, what questions we're asking, and who we invite. Who else could be involved in helping us solve these problems or creating this opportunity?

You wrote a Harvard Business Review *article titled "When TED Lost Control of Its Crowd." That's a very interesting example of this social dimension at work. Talk us through what happened with TED and the lessons from that.*

TED invited many people to give talks and run events using its brand. But some of what was co-created wasn't quite in line with what TED wanted in the marketplace. What should they do? Instead of taking the person who was responsible behind the woodshed, they actually made it a public social act of how we can solve this problem.

They started by saying yes, there's a problem, and then to everyone who had been a critic they said, How would you help us solve it? And they started co-opting even their worst critics into the process.

What was interesting was the social dynamic. To begin with people said, "Just tell us what you want us to do to fix the problem." But TED said we're not going to tell you the specifics of what to do because all that teaches you is to come back and ask more questions. Actually, we're going to celebrate the things that work and show you. So we're going to amplify and reflect back to you what is good. We're going to show you what's good and reward the best of the best so that you can see an example of what it looks like, and you can duplicate that example.

Throughout that whole process people kept trying to throw the ball back to TED. This is the real dilemma of social leadership. There are parallels with being a parent. If you are a parent, you will recognize this little behavior. I remember a time when I asked my son to set the dinner table. He came back with questions, I don't know, 100 times over the course of six months. Do I have to put water on the table? Do I have to put the fork in this spot? He kept asking specific questions.

A big part of me wanted to say this is not worth it; I'll just put the fork down myself. I wanted to stop answering the questions. But it was better to say, You figure it out. What did you do yesterday? And how would you learn this? What Google video could he pull up? Why don't you ask other people what a good place setting looks like? And I just kept throwing the ball back to him, and so the learning system was happening inside him and didn't rely on me. I was teaching him to learn and making him stronger in the process.

TED did exactly the same thing. Every time somebody said, Hey, can you guys just stipulate stuff? TED said, It's not *my* problem. In other words, this is not TED corporate's problem. This is *our* collective problem, and we're going to solve it together, and then you guys are going to reinforce it and enforce it among yourselves so that we own it together.

Are you saying that this is a different style of leadership—social leadership?

Yes, it's social leadership. It's like the ball stays in the court, being run by the team. And then you just teach them how to do better plays so that they can start to get higher and higher performance professionally. Community managers start and then colead with you, and they start to establish the standard, and manage the standard, and raise the standard. Those are ways in which sometimes we fail the test when we're switching over to a different model of leadership. We think, Oh, well, they can't do it.

The reason they keep coming back to me is that they can't do it, so I'd better go back to that sort of more directed approach. But really it's just a little social test to give them more tools, show them what good looks like. Reward that behavior, encourage them to learn among themselves, because that's the principle you're trying to get duplicated so that it scales without you as a leader having to do it for them.

What are the skills required to lead a crowd in that way? It sounds time-consuming.

It's both time-consuming and not time-consuming because what corporate leaders are largely doing today is inefficient and time-consuming in its own way. Things are going up and down a chain of command, being rolled up, vetted, rolled up again, vetted some more, approved by someone, and rolled back down, and by the time it gets back, the situation may have changed. Leaders are trying to go faster and faster in that corporate hierarchical structure only because they can't keep up with the rate of market change.

Personally, as a leader I don't want to spend that much time approving or disapproving things, and I don't think you do either. It's a very slow and tiring process. But how about I share with you in some public forums the criteria by which we want to operate or what the horizon that we're all aiming for is? You guys figure it out. You're smart, intelligent people—figure it out. Then as a leader I've figured out how to get everyone solving problems and identifying opportunities.

An example I've seen that I think is a good one is Google. Google has an interweb where it posts strategies at the very top levels, divisionwide, and so on. People ask questions and critique the company's strategy. In fact, there have been some comments like "I hate this strategy." People feel comfortable saying anything and everything in this forum.

Questions get asked, conversations end up happening, clarity gets discovered. It's that kind of thing. When a product manager wants to do this or that, the leader asks, "How does this fit with the strategy?" Thus, the burden is on that one question. It isn't on the leader to determine whether an idea matches the strategy. The burden is on the thousand product managers to figure out what fits.

Of course, the leader's role then is to ask more questions, to advise, to teach, and so it's different.

I'm not sure it's harder, but it's definitely different. In the long run you can have more participants actually using their brainpower.

Ultimately, you're saying it's a better way; it's going to be a more productive way of reaching solutions.
For sure. The reason I wrote the TED article is that this is what modern leadership looks like. TED corporate now hosts three events a year with a staff that I think is up to 120 people, and they have to handle corporate sponsorships and so on. But over 6,000 events have happened on their behalf, curating tons of ideas that matter, finding the best leaders. How could such a small organization do 6,000 events in a conventional business way? You couldn't possibly tap into the talent pool and the creativity of someone in Houston, Texas, or a slum outside Nairobi, Kenya.

What I'm saying is that openness leads to scale, openness leads to new ideas I couldn't have thought of by myself. And by the way, even if 120 people in America could come up with all those ideas, they would be coming out of a largely American-centric point of view rather than a global point of view. How do we become an organization in which a great idea, regardless of its origin, matters? How do you allow that filtering process?

Is this a fundamental shift in human organization? Does the new technology allow us to create a social process that was impossible before? Does this mark

*a watershed for humankind? Are we going to do
things differently?*
I think we are, and I think we want to go there. If you
think back to a couple of hundred years ago, we had
artisan-type work. You were a book writer or a crafts-
man, and your efficiency at reaching scale was poor.
Then we moved into the industrial era, in which we
got efficiency but lost the artisan talent that each of us
could bring.

Now networks mean that companies can actually allow individual perspective and creativity and
individual talent to come back, but without losing
the ability to have scale. I think that's where we are
with this tectonic shift. It's something that all human
beings have and desire: the ability to have their ideas
and creativity matter. They want to have their own art
show up in the world. They want to use and showcase
their individual talents, whatever they are.

*Where are we now with this social revolution? How
far into it are we? Do we have critical mass?*
We're probably 10 years in. We've had 10 years with
enough cognitive surplus and with the ability to do
this connectivity stuff. But probably only in the last
three years can you see something where you can make
money at it. You can organize all that stuff pretty efficiently, so that's why TED is an interesting case.

There are a couple of other examples of organizations. However, we're at a very early stage, which is
why my social era book is a hypothesis. I said I can't

prove this to you yet because there's not enough evidence, but I'm going to use the weak signal to suggest there's a directional shift. The question is: When does everyone do this?

Bill Gates said that with the impact of all the new technology we overestimate the change that will occur in the next 2 years and underestimate the change that will occur in the next 10. I think that's true, so we shouldn't let ourselves be lulled into inaction by saying it's far away. But building it into a business model and building it into really viable leadership constructs could take 20 years for us to see the results.

Do you see anything that could derail it, or is this inevitable?
Things could definitely derail it. There are a couple of things that you can point to right now that nobody knows the answer to. One is that way too many people are working for free. The idea that all of us can do the work together, blah, blah, blah, is really interesting. The dark side of this is that if you look at those 6,000 people who created TED events, most of them didn't earn any money from that.

It gave them more media attention, gave them maybe more impact, all those things, yes, but sometimes people have got to buy shoes and feed the kids. We have to wrap the economic balance point around that, and until that's fixed, I think we're going to continue to really struggle. The other issue is that everyone tends to look at these social initiatives and ask why they failed. Why did Occupy Wall Street fail? Why did the Arab Spring fail?

Some people will say the Arab Spring succeeded. But I think we had one dictator and now we have a different one, and so we didn't really see a big change in allowing people's voices to come forward and create a new result. Thus, the question is about whether we can really effect change, tectonic change, not just the appearance of change. How can we get to outcomes we want, not just feel better for a while? There are very few signals that we're there yet.

That's the area where we need to see more evidence in order to make forward motion.

For the managers of the world who are reading this interview, what should they take away from your thinking, from your ideas?

It's time to get ready. I might get only 50 percent of these futuristic ideas right, but I couldn't tell you which 50 percent. But directionally, this is the horizon to go toward. I'd have you open up your thinking in two directions.

The first one is to stop thinking about your organization as a closed system. How do you invite others in, whether it's a customer or a partner or whatever? How do you break down those silos within your organization to allow all talent to play regardless of where people are in the world, regardless of whether they work for you? So openness around talent is one thing.

The second challenge is to stop thinking about what you're producing as a thing. You make a thing and sell it is old-school. Instead, you have to start thinking more about how you enable many other participants to start building things with you. And so you move from IBM makes servers to IBM knows how to make servers and has lots of other useful knowledge and expertise, and it doesn't matter who makes the actual thing of servers or other things.

IBM becomes more powerful because it can be the glue. It can ask the right questions, can solve different problems. So think about how to build more of a platform mentality rather than a product mentality.

Those two vectors seem to me to be the most important. All growth and performance can be tied to opening up those two vectors and moving from transactional ways of selling things to relational and ultimately connected ways of selling things where it's not even about did I make it or did you make it.

What advice would you give your 10-year-old son who has his whole career ahead of him and is trying to find a place in the world?

He's going to have a chance to think not just about how to fit into an existing structure but how to create a structure that works for him, that's right for him. We're going to think less about having a job and more about a portfolio of things that we are interested in doing and figure out how you put together the economics behind that.

That's one thing. The second is to understand that who you work with isn't limited by geography. It isn't limited by who you already know. You can actually start working with strangers, and they can start helping you solve problems. You can learn how to find them, and how to work with them, and how to negotiate that framework of your shared purpose. Kids growing up today do this instinctively, and so actually my son probably teaches me as much about collaboration as I can teach him.

Notes

Introduction

1. David A. Garvin, "How Google Sold Its Engineers on Management," *Harvard Business Review*, December 2013.
2. Joseph Schumpeter, "Measuring Management," *The Economist*, January 18, 2014.

Chapter 1

1. Tobias Preis, Helen Susannah Moat, and H. Eugene Stanley, "Quantifying Trading Behavior in Financial Markets," Nature Publishing Group Scientific Reports, April 2013.
2. All quotes are from interviews unless otherwise noted.
3. Alex Gregory, "Golden Lessons," *Business Strategy Review*, Winter 2013.

Chapter 3

1. Antionette Schoar and Marianne Bertrand, "Managing with Style: The Effect of Managers on Corporate Policy," *Quarterly Journal of Economics*, November 2003.

Chapter 5

1. Sun Tzu, *The Art of War* (trans. Griffiths), Oxford University Press, 1963.

Acknowledgments

This book celebrates a collection of thinkers who we believe will shape the business future. Their ideas are fresh, compelling, and practical. We hope you enjoy meeting them as much as we did.

We would like to thank all the thinkers featured in the book and those we interviewed.

In particular, thanks are due to James Allworth, Laurence Capron, Dorie Clark, Adam Grant, Monika Hamori, Ioannis Ioannou, Dame Ellen MacArthur, Nilofer Merchant, Ethan Mollick, Lee Newman, Gianpiero Petriglieri, Navi Radjou, and Christian Stadler.

Index

About
the Authors

Stuart Crainer and Des Dearlove create and champion business ideas. Stuart and Des are the creators of the Thinkers50 (www.thinkers50.com), the original global ranking of business thought leaders. Their work in this area led *Management Today* to describe them as "market makers par excellence."

Stuart and Des are former columnists at *The (London) Times*, contributing editors to the American magazine *Strategy+Business*, and editors of the bestselling *Financial Times Handbook of Management*. Their books include *The Management Century*, *Gravy Training*, *The Future of Leadership*, and *Generation Entrepreneur*. These books are available in more than 20 languages.

Stuart is the editor of the award-winning *Business Strategy Review*. *Personnel Today* has selected him as one of the most influential people in British people management. Des is an associate fellow of the Saïd Business School at Oxford University and is the author of a bestselling study of the leadership style of Richard Branson. Stuart and Des are adjunct professors at IE Business School.

About The Thinkers50

The Thinkers50 is the definitive global ranking of management thinkers. Its mission is to scan, rank, and share the best business thinking. First published in 2001, the Thinkers50 has been published every two years since then. The ranking was topped in 2011 and 2013 by Harvard Business School's Professor Clayton Christensen. The previous winners were C. K. Prahalad (2009 and 2007), Michael Porter (2005), and Peter Drucker (2003 and 2001).

The ranking is based on voting at the Thinkers50 website and input from a team of advisors led by Stuart Crainer and Des Dearlove. The Thinkers50 has 10 established criteria by which thinkers are evaluated:

- Originality of ideas
- Practicality of ideas
- Presentation style
- Written communication
- Loyalty of followers
- Business sense
- International outlook
- Rigor of research
- Impact of ideas
- Power to inspire

Business strategies from
THE WORLD'S MOST ELITE
BUSINESS THINKERS

FEATURING
DAN PINK • ROSABETH MOSS KANTER
LYNDA GRATTON • TAMMY ERICKSON

THINKERS 50

Management
Cutting-Edge Thinking to Engage and
Motivate Your Employees for Success

STUART CRAINER • DES DEARLOVE

FEATURING
W. CHAN KIM AND RENÉE MAUBORGNE
ROGER MARTIN • C.K. PRAHALAD
RICHARD D'AVENI

THINKERS 50

Strategy
The Art and Science of
Strategy Creation and Execution

STUART CRAINER • DES DEARLOVE

FEATURING
DON TAPSCOTT • CLAY CHRISTENSEN
VIJAY GOVINDARAJAN • GARY HAMEL
LINDA HILL

THINKERS 50

Innovation
Breakthrough Thinking to Take Your
Business to the Next Level

STUART CRAINER • DES DEARLOVE

FEATURING
JIM COLLINS • WARREN BENNIS
BARBARA KELLERMAN
MARSHALL GOLDSMITH

THINKERS 50

Leadership
Organizational Success Through Leadership

STUART CRAINER • DES DEARLOVE

FEATURING
HEIDI GRANT HALVORSON • LIZ WISEMAN
CARMEN CANNON • CHARLENE PETRIGGERS

THINKERS 50

Future Thinkers
New Thinking on Leadership, Strategy
and Innovation for the 21st Century

STUART CRAINER • DES DEARLOVE

FEATURING
RAM CHARAN • SUMANTRA GHOSHAL
NITIN NOHRIA • AND MORE

THINKERS 50

**Business Thought Leaders
From India**
The Best Ideas on Innovation, Management,
Strategy, and Leadership

STUART CRAINER • DES DEARLOVE

www.thinkers50.com

Available in print and eBook

Learn More. Do More.
MHPROFESSIONAL.COM